UWEM ESSIA

ECONOMIC GOVERNANCE AND PUBLIC FINANCE DYNAMICS

Public Expenditure Policy and the Path to Sustainable Development

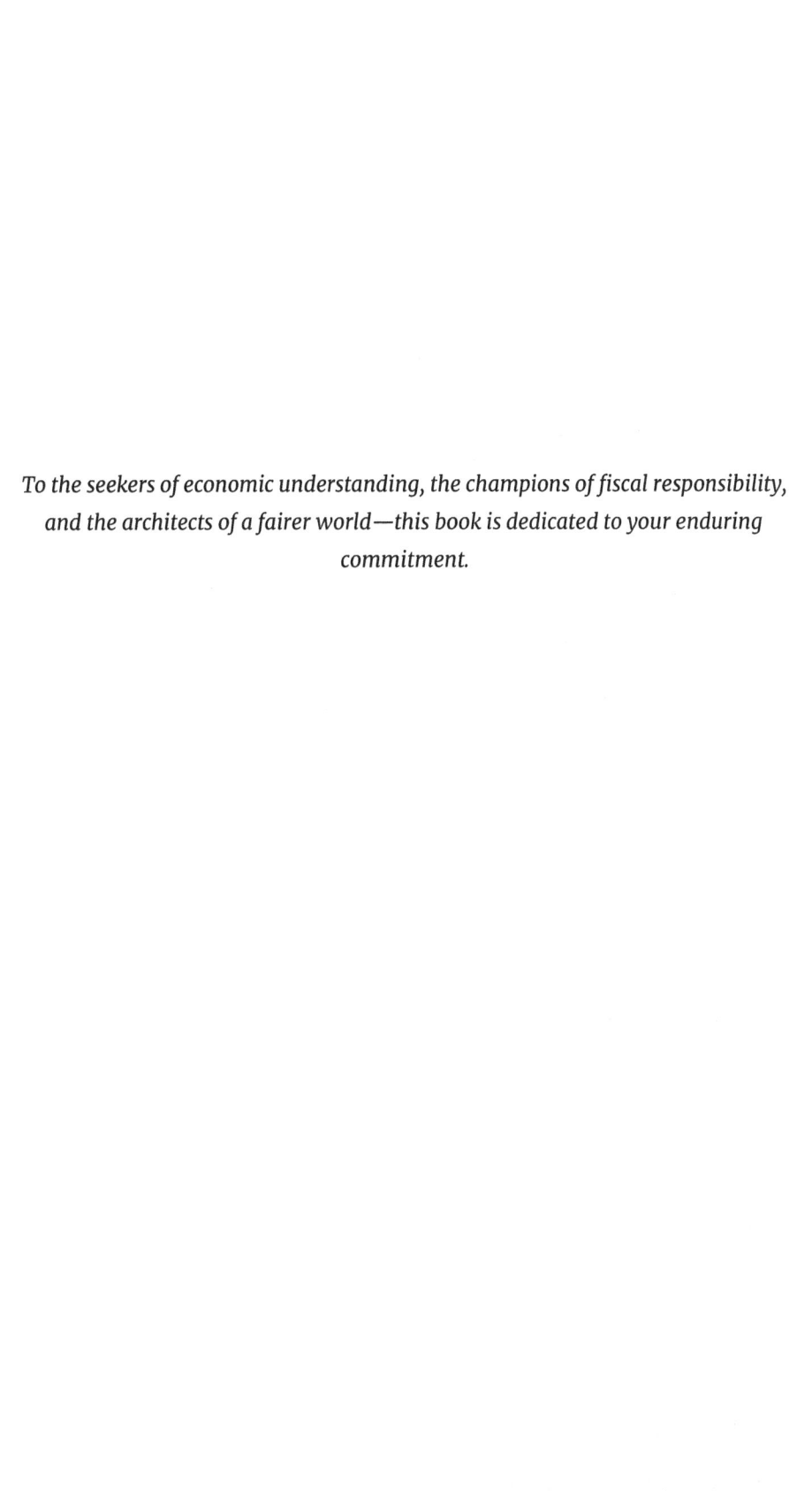

To the seekers of economic understanding, the champions of fiscal responsibility, and the architects of a fairer world—this book is dedicated to your enduring commitment.

Contents

Preface

The book, "Economic Governance and Public Finance Dynamics" explores the multifaceted dynamics that shape contemporary thinking on the state's role in economic development. From the foundational principles of public goods and government intervention to the intricacies of fiscal policy, fiscal federalism, and the role of budgets in economic development, each chapter unfolds a critical aspect of our political-economic fabric.

Navigating Economic Inequality: Chapter One dissects the essence of public goods and the imperatives of government intervention, confronting the challenges posed by free ridership, externalities, and conditional public goods. The transformative potential of public goods, particularly contingently public goods, emerges as a beacon for addressing economic injustices.

Contingently Public Goods and Political Feasibility: Chapter Two explains the complex terrain of economic inequality that transcends income distribution concerns. Contingently, public goods emerge as a strategic instrument to foster equality, emphasizing their efficiency and political feasibility. Regulatory and property rights approaches offer pathways to ensure fair distribution, challenging traditional notions of economic balance.

A Symphony of Allocation, Distribution, and Stabilization: Chapter Three orchestrates the symphony of fiscal policy, scrutinizing its role in wealth and income distribution, from optimal distribution to the intersection of fiscal and monetary instruments, the challenges and conflicts inherent in these multifaceted functions are dissected. The coordination or conflict of objectives in fiscal policy unfolds as a dynamic challenge in pursuit of economic equilibrium.

Fiscal Federalism - Harmonizing Revenue, Expenditure, and Equity: In Chapter Four, we embark on a journey through fiscal federalism, unraveling the complexities of taxable capacity and the equalization of fiscal positions. The delicate balance between central and decentralized responsibilities comes to the forefront, offering insights into addressing benefit spillovers and fiscal differentials. Equity advantages of central taxes become a focal point, challenging conventional wisdom on fiscal decentralization.

Budgets, Debt, Taxation, and Economic Development: Chapter Five illuminates the origins, features, and objectives of budgets, exploring their pivotal role in resource reallocation, redistribution, and stabilization. The burden transfer through debt financing unfolds as a crucial aspect, provoking contemplation on intergenerational equity. Also, the linkages of fiscal stability, growth, and resource allocation in less developed countries are examined, showcasing the pivotal role of fiscal policy in shaping economic trajectories.

Theories, Perspectives, and Evaluation Frameworks: Chapter Seven takes us through the evolving landscape of public expenditure, from historical perspectives to contemporary challenges. The growth of democracy, population dynamics, and the impact of wars and foreign aid become crucial factors shaping public spending. Theories from Adolph Wagner to the Peacock-Wiseman hypothesis provide a lens to understand the forces propelling public expenditure growth. As we delve into the evaluation frameworks, the macro-level assessment, consolidation of deficits, and functional composition analysis offer a comprehensive understanding of the complexities involved.

Cost-Benefit Analysis, Public Expenditure, and Debt Dynamics: Our journey concludes in Chapter Eight, explaining the cost-benefit analysis for government projects and the logic behind government intervention. The impact of public expenditure on economic development takes center stage, emphasizing its role in minimizing adverse effects, reducing inequalities, and stabilizing economies during fluctuations. The economics of debt financing becomes a prism through which we understand governments' nuanced decisions in balancing revenue and expenditure.

In weaving these chapters, Economic Governance and Public Finance Dynamics aims to be a guiding beacon for scholars, policymakers, and curious minds, providing insights into the intricate interplay of economic principles that underpin our societies.

INTRODUCTION

Welcome to a compelling exploration of economic intricacies in "Economic Governance and Public Finance Dynamics." In the following pages, we embark on a riveting journey through the interconnected realms of public goods, government intervention, fiscal policy, and the captivating interaction of economic forces. As we delve into the chapters, each unfolds a vibrant exposition of economic principles, revealing the challenges and opportunities that shape our societies, from the transformative potential of public goods to the strategic role of contingently public goods in addressing economic inequalities.

This book aims to enlighten readers seeking a profound understanding of public expenditure and economic governance, and how they impact development. It equally explores the complex landscape of fiscal federalism, bringing to life the delicate balance between revenue, expenditure, and equity, exploring the foundational role of budgets, debt, and taxation in economic development, and unraveling the threads that weave our economic destinies around the state.

Economic Governance and Public Finance Dynamics invites us to decipher the theories, perspectives, and evaluation frameworks that underpin public expenditure. From historical perspectives to contemporary challenges, this book offers a comprehensive lens through which we can understand the forces propelling economic growth and development. Let us immerse ourselves in the world of cost-benefit analysis, public expenditure dynamics, and strategic decisions of governments. Welcome to an intellectual adventure—a journey that challenges assumptions sparks conversations and provides profound insights into the symphony of economic forces governing our world.

CHAPTER ONE: PUBLIC GOODS, INEQUALITY, AND GOVERNMENT INTERVENTION

Summary of Key Points

1. Public Goods Definition: Public goods are non-excludable and nonrivalrous commodities or services accessible to all members of society. Examples include national defense and clean air, but the challenge of free ridership often leads to over-provision.

2. Government Intervention Necessity: Understanding public goods and market failures underscores the need for government intervention in economic systems. Public goods, being nonrivalrous and non-excludable, face challenges such as the free-rider problem, necessitating government involvement for efficient provision.

3. Market Failures and Externalities: Market failures, resulting in inefficient distribution, may arise due to the absence of property rights. Externalities, either positive or negative, occur when one person's actions impact another's well-being, and these costs and benefits are not reflected in market prices.

4. Conditional Public Goods: Distinguishing between inherently public goods and contingently public goods is crucial. Contingently, public goods, which could be provided as club goods, raise questions about the fair distribution of benefits and compensation.

5. Benefit Principles and Distributive Justice: Examining benefit principles in providing public goods reveals unequal access, regressive compensation, and intrinsic disvaluation challenges. Proponents of social justice theories propose substantive criteria for just distribution.

6. Public Goods' Transformative Potential: Public goods, especially contingently public goods, can address economic injustices by diminishing the significance of private resource access to opportunities. Transforming club goods into public goods can express a commitment to inclusiveness.

Public Goods and Services

Public goods are commodities or services available to all members of society. These goods are non-excludable and nonrivalrous, meaning individuals cannot be excluded from their benefits, and one person's consumption does not diminish availability for others. Classic examples include national defense and clean air. However, public goods often need help with the challenge of free riders benefiting without contributing, leading to potential under-provision in the market due to non-payment exclusion. Understanding these concepts is crucial for policymakers and economists.

The concepts of public goods and market failures highlight the need for government intervention to make the economic system function efficiently. Generally, public goods must be nonrivalrous and non-excludable. Nonrivalrous means supply does not dwindle as consumption increases, and non-excludable means the good is available to all citizens. The free-rider problem arises when individuals benefit without contributing, such as those who do not pay taxes but still benefit from public goods. The opposite is private goods, which are both excludable and rivalrous, like a wedding ring or a slice of pizza.

Countries decide which goods and services are public based on national budgets. For example, many invest heavily in national defense, viewing it as a crucial public good. Some countries also treat social services like healthcare and public education as public goods, financing them through taxpayer funds.

Advocates argue that government spending on public goods has economic and social benefits, such as improved workforce participation and reduced poverty. Critics, however, argue that it can burden taxpayers and that private sectors could provide these goods more efficiently.

Market Failures, Public Goods, and Externalities

Market failure refers to an economic situation with inefficient distribution of goods and services in the free market, which occurs when individual incentives for rational behavior do not lead to rational outcomes for the group. In other words, decisions that may be correct for individuals collectively result in the wrong outcomes for the group. Traditional microeconomics illustrates this as a steady-state disequilibrium where the quantity supplied does not equal the quantity demanded. Market failures can occur due to the absence of property rights and costly negotiations. The Coase Theorem, introduced by economist Ronald Coase, challenges the conventional view by proposing that parties could reach mutually beneficial agreements without legal liability for externalities if transaction costs were low.

Externalities arise when one person's actions affect another's well-being, and these costs and benefits are not reflected in market prices. A positive externality occurs when, for example, my neighbors benefit from my yard cleanup, but I cannot charge them for it, potentially leading to less frequent cleaning. On the other hand, a negative externality arises when one person's actions, like pollution from a factory, harm others without proper consideration of the costs imposed.

Positive externalities are benefits that cannot be feasibly charged to provide, while negative externalities are costs that are impractical to charge not to provide. Despite the self-interested nature of markets, externalities undermine the social benefits of individual actions. For instance, if selfish consumers do not have to pay producers for benefits, they will not pay, leading to the failure of valuable products to appear. Research and development exemplify positive externalities, while air pollution represents a negative externality. Many economic arguments for government intervention stem from the belief that the market cannot efficiently provide public goods or handle externalities. Public health, education, national defense, and a clean environment are all considered public goods.

Non-excludability and Nonrivalrous Consumption: Public goods, characterized by nonexcludability and nonrivalrous consumption, present challenges. Nonexcludability means it is cost-prohibitive to prevent non-payers from enjoying the benefits, potentially leading to unproduced goods. Market failures can also result from government actions, such as subsidies or inadequate intellectual property protection. For instance, national defense is considered a public good because its consumption by one person does not reduce availability for others. Also, deciding which school to attend goes beyond the individual because the state may have preferences for how citizens should be educated, prompting a broader discussion on the state's role in market activities and the justification for government intervention. Generally, externalities can be problematic for markets, deviating from the idealized equilibrium of perfectly competitive models. For instance, the argument against smoking regulations shifted in the 1990s, incorporating welfare economics and externalities to explain market failures in maximizing social welfare.

A major instance of market failure is greenhouse gas emissions. If artificial global warming is correct, policymakers face a massive negative externality as activities contributing to increased greenhouse gas concentrations do not account for potential harm imposed on others. When markets fail, competitive enterprises may theoretically produce the largest income from given resources, but real economies fall short of this ideal, resulting in net losses to society. The justification for government intervention often stems from market failures related to production or distribution. Public goods, freely accessible to all members of the public, create a dilemma due to their non-excludable nature. This market failure, known as the public goods dilemma, necessitates taxation. The moral limits of markets are explored by philosophers like Debra Satz, who argues against allowing some markets, such as organ sales, to operate freely.

The Macroeconomic Context of Market Failure

A classic application of market failure is demonstrated in the Keynesian remedy for unemployment. Keynes suggested that during economic downturns, the government should step in and fill the role of businesses by investing in public works and hiring the unemployed. The Keynesian remedy contrasts the neoclassical economics theory for the demand and supply of private goods, which economists conventionally rely on while answering questions about what goods to produce, how to organize resources, and how to distribute final goods and services. The Keynesian position emphasizes the importance of institutions and the need for government to act decisively beyond the market. However, despite recognizing the fact or reality of "market failure" in economics, scholars have been reluctant to adopt an adequate model, perhaps due to the analytical complexity that modeling government institutions would present. The focus has primarily been on micro- and macro-level market corrections, neglecting political institutions. Ironically, public-choice pioneers attempting to introduce practical realism into political behavior models faced criticism for alleged ideological bias. The persistent myth of a benevolent despot continues to influence perceptions of political authority.

Conditional Public Goods

The significance of conditional public goods has recently garnered increased attention from philosophers. A distinction is proposed between inherently public goods and contingently public goods. Inherently, public goods are nonrivalrous and non-excludable, while contingently, public goods, provided in a non-exclusionary form, are nonrivalrous but can be excluded by choice. The qualification "as a matter of choice" emphasizes the intentional nature of providing goods in a non-exclusionary form, preventing confusion arising from the inherent non-excludability of public goods. The term "non-exclusionary form" is interpreted broadly, encompassing goods accessible for free or with a token charge easily affordable to every individual.

Distinguishing between inherently and contingently public goods is crucial as it helps separate intentional choices in providing goods from market failures due to the inability to exclude others. Thus, economists now try to distinguish between 'public goods' and 'publicized goods.' According to Vaughn Bryan Baltzly and Anomaly, publicized goods result from a policy decision to make private goods freely available voluntarily or via government mandates.

It is essential to note that the distinction between "public goods" and publicized goods" is more of demarcating a spectrum rather than a strict divide, as few goods are inherently non-excludable, and the cost of exclusion may vary. Also, the non-excludability of goods, making them inherently public, depends on technology and may change over time. Moreover, few goods are entirely nonrivalrous or non-excludable, and the criterion of non-rivalry should be interpreted flexibly, distinguishing between more pure or impure public goods based on their degree of rivalry. There are also comparable distinctions between universal and non-universal public goods and essential and discretionary public goods.

Distributive Justice and the Provision of Contingently Public Goods

In recent philosophical discussions on public goods, a key focus has been on the ideal theory level, specifically examining the criteria for justly distributing burdens and benefits associated with public goods provision. Discussions are centered on two key issues. The first concerns unequal access to club goods to the extent that it can be contextualized as the unacceptable transfer payments to the affluent. The second point relates to the intrinsic devaluation of public goods, which may lead to unacceptable transfers to those who disvalue the inclusive mode of provision. Both viewpoints relate to contingently public goods, specifically those whose provision is not directly mandated by justice and is discretionary.

Two observations drive examining justice demands in the provision of public goods. Firstly, public goods essential for justice, such as the rule of law, are necessary for restraining arbitrary power. Secondly, there are goods not mandated by justice but raise justice-related concerns in their provision. These are termed "discretionary public goods." Proponents of social justice theories have primarily focused on procedural criteria when considering discretionary public goods, but these approaches often need to be revised in addressing distributive justice. In response to procedural limitations, some authors advocate substantive criteria, proposing a two-step approach: first, addressing essential public goods according to justice principles, and second, determining the distribution of costs and benefits for discretionary public goods.

The benefit principle, ensuring benefits for everyone, is considered basic but permissive. More restrictive principles include the proportional benefit principle, suggesting contributions proportional to individual benefits, and the equal benefit principle, aiming to equalize net benefits. Critics have raised concerns about these principles. For instance, the proportional benefit principle has been criticized for resembling an enterprise model and contradicting the idea of equal stakeholding in a political community. While avoiding certain problems, the equal benefit principle is criticized for its strictness, potentially prohibiting public goods provision even when it would harm no one and benefit many. Moreover, the proportional benefit principle is considered complete, needing more guidance when multiple sets of discretionary public goods satisfy proportionality. While addressing this issue, the equal benefit principle is vulnerable to a leveling-down objection, which could be mitigated through transfer schemes.

Challenges Arising from Contingently Public Goods

Public goods raise two critical objections that simultaneously challenge various benefit principles. The first objection stems from the unequal access to club goods. Since public goods can be provided as club goods contingently, an uneven distribution of private resources can result in disparate access to these club goods. This inequality influences the distribution of benefits when these goods are provided as public goods, leading to seemingly implausible transfers to the individually wealthy. Consider a public swimming pool as an illustrative example. While it may be initially perceived as a public good benefiting all swimmers, a financially privileged individual with access to a private fitness club offering pool access might claim that the public pool does not benefit her. According to the benefits principles, this could lead to counterintuitive conclusions, such as her being owed compensation.

Examining the case further, if the affluent swimmer retains her club membership without utilizing the public pool, benefit principles imply compensatory payments to her, even if there is a surplus benefit from the public pool. This appears perplexing, raising questions about compensating individuals who do not directly benefit from public goods provision. While considerations of justice may vary based on individual cases, the challenge lies in reconciling compensatory claims with the notion of an initially just distribution of private goods.

In evaluating the implications, it becomes crucial to distinguish between cases where an initial distribution is deemed just and instances where transfer payments to the wealthy seem implausible. The argument emphasizes the need for cautious judgment, acknowledging that our intuitions about specific cases may influence decisions. However, as the discussion operates at the level of ideal theory, it aims to avoid being swayed by intuitions rooted in nonideal circumstances. The central question remains: Can a group committed to making a good freely available to everyone be reasonably obligated to fund compensation for wealthy individuals who, while preferring an equivalent club good, are not negatively affected? The tension lies in determining the appropriateness of compensating those who receive less benefit due to pre-existing access to club goods in a context of initially just resource allocation. A pragmatic argument against compensating the affluent who prefer an equivalent club good is that they need to contribute the value due to their non-participation as their responsibility to ensure a more peaceful society by helping the poorer members.

Challenging the Benefit Principles: Regressive Compensation and Intrinsic Disvaluation

The argument against the benefits principles, stemming from unequal access to club goods, brings to light a significant flaw—namely, the principles demand highly regressive compensation in the context of providing public goods. This critique goes beyond Claassen's position, which focuses on preferences for public versus market goods, by highlighting wealth inequalities as a central concern. Specifically, the argument contends that the starting point of a pure market society disproportionately disadvantages the less wealthy, as they stand to gain more from the provision of contingently public goods in comparison to a pure market economy.

Moreover, this argument explicitly distinguishes between inherently and contingently public goods. Contingently, public goods, which could have been provided as club goods, reveal the implausibly regressive distributive demands of the benefit principles due to unequal initial access to such club goods. Unlike Claassen's more moderate conclusion suggesting "meta-neutrality," the argument presented here asserts that the benefit principles are implausible, especially given their benchmark of a pure market economy, as they necessitate highly regressive compensation for the provision of contingently public goods. Another objection arises from the intrinsic disvaluation of public goods. The benefit principles, surprisingly, mandate compensation to individuals who devalue the provision of contingently public goods solely because they disvalue their inclusive mode of provision. While Claassen's argument questions the assumed neutrality toward individual preferences, this objection delves into the distinction between the specific good provided and its mode of provision. This distinction is crucial because a market could offer goods like parks as club goods, and individuals can value or disvalue a good for itself and its mode of provision.

The possibility of intrinsically disvaluing public goods poses a challenge to the principles of benefits, and its precise form hinges on the interpretation of the principle of neutrality underlying them. Embedded in a liberal framework demanding neutrality toward citizens' preferences, the benefit principles lack explicit qualifications. A literal interpretation of neutrality raises an objection based on intrinsic disvaluation, exemplified by a person A objecting to public parks due to perceived class distinctions. However, this objection is nuanced, and the benefit principles need qualifications to exclude instances of intrinsic disvaluation that contradict the spirit of a political community founded on equality.

Reevaluating the Principle of Neutrality and Intrinsic Disvaluation

An important juncture arises when considering alternative interpretations of the principle of neutrality. Some argue that a literal, unqualified interpretation—remaining neutral toward all preferences—may be too naïve, implicitly requiring the exclusion of at least some immoral preferences. This perspective contends that the example presented earlier, involving person Z's objection to public parks, is moralized and should be dismissed because Z's preference is based on immoral classist views. This leads to the question: Can we find a non-moralized example where a person's intrinsic disvaluation of a public good does not warrant compensation?

Exploring this question, it is crucial to note that rejecting immoral preferences as part of the principle of neutrality does not prescribe a specific alternative. Three interpretations emerge: (ii) demanding neutrality toward all preferences except those implicitly deemed immoral, (iii) demanding neutrality toward all preferences except those proven to be immoral, and (iv) stipulating that a preference is immoral if and only if neutrality need not be maintained. Interpretation (iv) categorically rules out non-moralized examples, as any preference not warranting compensation is inherently labeled immoral. However, interpretations (ii) and (iii), which carry substantive claims, open the possibility of non-moralized examples.

Consider person Y, residing in an egalitarian republic, who disfavors public parks not due to class or racist views but simply because she prefers private goods. Y's case contrasts with Z's, as Y's intrinsic disvaluation is not grounded in morally tainted beliefs. While B's preference is not inherently immoral, the argument maintains that Y's disvaluation should be disregarded when assessing public park provision benefits. This is because, being an indoors person, Y's ability to enjoy public parks remains unaffected by their universal accessibility. If this argument holds, Y's case is a non-moralized example under interpretations (ii) and (iii), suggesting that the benefit principles must be circumscribed. However, even if one disputes this, the broader point remains—proponents of benefit principles must address conditions under which intrinsic disvaluation of public goods is considered immoral and can be ignored. This issue is complex, as intrinsic disvaluation does not universally appear immoral; for instance, vulnerable groups may rightly seek exclusive spaces. The challenge persists: When is intrinsic disvaluation an immoral preference deserving dismissal, and why? This question gains significance in scenarios where individuals may never use or notice the public goods, raising ethical considerations for specific cases like religious objections to the universal accessibility of sacred sites.

Public Goods' Potential to Tackle Injustices

The argument asserts their transformative potential in the broader context of public goods. The provision of public goods can diminish the significance of economic inequalities, lessening the impact of private resource access on opportunities. This, at times, presents an attractive alternative to transfer-based policies. While public goods might not universally achieve this effect and could even exacerbate existing injustices, their potential to act as an equalizing force is noteworthy. Specifically focusing on contingent public goods, the ability to convert a club well into a contingent public good efficiently addresses injustices, especially when this transformation involves removing restrictions on club good access. The following points are pertinent:

Cost-Efficiency in Provision: Contingently public goods, potentially cost-less under specific conditions, can sidestep the common objection of market interference.

Expressing Commitment to Inclusiveness: As goods that could have been club goods, the public provision of contingently public goods becomes a potent expression of a commitment to inclusiveness, vital in combating status inequalities.

Diminishing Club Goods' Relevance: By undermining the relevance of club goods, contingently public goods pave the way for greater equality of opportunity, dismantling a crucial barrier.

Addressing Economic Injustices

Turning to economic inequalities, the argument acknowledges that not all economic disparities are inherently unjust. Recognizing justified inequalities or those rooted in deservedness, the focus narrows to those genuinely constituting injustices. Traditional measures like the Gini coefficient provide insights into economic inequality but fall short of highlighting the role of private material resource ownership. The importance of such ownership fluctuates based on societal structures. A critical determinant is the extent to which a society provides public goods. While quantifying the importance of private resource ownership or the prevalence of public goods remains complex, both aspects warrant attention when evaluating economic inequality. Solely scrutinizing the distribution of private resources overlooks the societal configurations that either amplify or mitigate the necessity for private resource ownership to access valuable goods. Therefore, a nuanced concern for economic inequality extends beyond the mere distribution of resources.

Review Questions

1. How do public goods differ from private goods, and what challenges do public goods face regarding provision?
2. What is the role of government intervention in addressing market failures, and how do externalities contribute to inefficient market outcomes?
3. Explain the concept of contingent public goods and their significance in addressing economic inequalities.

4. What challenges arise in applying benefit principles to the provision of public goods, and how do these principles relate to distributive justice?
5. In what ways can public goods transform societal structures and contribute to a more equitable distribution of opportunities?
6. How does the distinction between inherently public goods and contingent public goods impact discussions about justice and compensation?

Discussion Points

1. Balancing Taxation and Public Goods Provision: Explore the trade-offs and considerations governments face when deciding on taxation to fund public goods. Discuss the potential economic and social benefits versus the concerns of taxpayers.
2. Ethical Considerations in Compensation for Unequal Access: Delve into the ethical implications of compensating individuals with unequal access to club goods when public goods are provided. Discuss the moral limits and societal obligations in such scenarios.
3. Public Goods as Agents of Social Transformation: Discuss the transformative potential of public goods in addressing economic inequalities. Explore specific examples where the provision of public goods can act as an equalizing force in society.

CHAPTER TWO: CONTINGENTLY PUBLIC GOODS AND CHECKING ECONOMIC INEQUALITY

Summary of Key Points

1. Economic Inequality Beyond Income Distribution: The chapter emphasizes that concerns about economic inequality should go beyond income and wealth distribution to encompass differences in people's capabilities. Providing contingently public goods can be an effective strategy to address such inequalities.

2. Efficiency of Contingently Public Goods: Public goods are proposed as an indirect yet efficient strategy to address economic inequality. The non-rivalrous nature of these goods allows for expanded accessibility without incurring additional costs, potentially surpassing the impact of traditional redistribution methods.

3. Political Feasibility: The universal availability of public goods, especially contingently public goods, is argued to enhance their political feasibility. This is due to the broader political support garnered by universally applicable programs compared to means-tested initiatives, encouraging wealthier individuals to support public goods provision through taxes.

4. Regulation and Property Rights: The chapter explores two methods to ensure the provision of contingently public goods without traditional taxation. One involves regulations prohibiting exclusion and transform-

ing club goods into public goods. The other relates to the assignment of property rights, where the initial allocation can determine whether goods remain public or become private.

5. Addressing Inequalities in Opportunity: Contingently, public goods are positioned to address inequalities in access and opportunity, offering alternatives to market consumption. The chapter presents scenarios where public goods provision can foster greater equality without solely relying on redistributive measures.

6. Free-Rider Problem: The free-rider problem is a market failure affecting public goods. The chapter delves into the economic efficiency effects of free-riding, particularly in scenarios where non-excludable goods are rivalrous, leading to overconsumption and potential resource depletion.

Tackling Economic Inequality: The Power of Public Goods

Concerns about economic inequality should extend beyond the mere distribution of income and wealth to encompass the differences in people's capabilities within the existing economic landscape. This perspective suggests that providing public goods can serve as an indirect strategy to address income and wealth inequalities by diminishing their relevance. Moreover, it posits that the outright provision of public goods might be more efficient and politically viable than traditional redistribution of private resources. Economically, the efficiency stems from the non-rivalrous nature of public goods. Their consumption by some does not significantly deplete availability for others. This inherent characteristic can lead to efficiency gains when providing goods as contingently public rather than club goods, expanding accessibility without incurring additional costs. This economic rationale suggests that progress toward economic equality concerning the differences in people's capabilities can be more effectively achieved by providing public goods, potentially surpassing the impact of taxation alone.

The universal availability of public goods can enhance their feasibility. The notion that benefits are extended universally tends to garner higher political support than means-tested programs. This dynamic may encourage the wealthy to be more receptive to financing public goods provision through taxes rather than contributing to targeted transfer payments. While this argument applies broadly to public goods, contingently, public goods stand out for their potential efficiency in this regard. Their efficiency lies in the possibility of transforming corresponding club goods into contingently public goods at negligible costs, thereby increasing access without detriment to anyone. Consider a scenario where a pay-TV channel operates in a society grappling with economic inequality. If this channel can be made universally accessible at no added expense, efficiency gains could be realized, especially if taxation is levied on willing subscribers at the current rate.

A hypothetical example illustrates this: A society with economic inequality centered around unequal access to pay TV might find that providing a lump sum subsidy to the TV channel, contingent on universal accessibility, is an efficient and feasible way to address economic inequality. This approach ensures widespread access more effectively than redistributive transfer payments. It may even be acceptable to existing subscribers, as they contribute to universal access without substantially increasing costs. However, this scenario is simplified and needs to account for practical complexities. The ability to tax those who subscribe to a channel is challenging, necessitating general tax revenue and potential objections from contributors. Moreover, subsidies eliminate market forces that drive channels to offer appealing content to attract subscribers.

When considering specific contingently public goods, evaluating the benefits and drawbacks becomes imperative. The justification for public provision hinges on how central access is to concerns about economic inequality. Public libraries may present a compelling case where economic inequalities limiting access to education are of greater concern than inequalities related to pay-TV access. Therefore, the provision of contingently public goods can be a targeted and effective strategy to address economic inequalities, albeit with the need for careful consideration in each case.

Furthermore, another distinctive feature of contingently public goods is their ability to, under certain circumstances, evade the common objection that public goods provision necessitates justification due to taxation. Both proponents and critics of public goods typically agree that unless secured through assurance contracts or funded by charities, public goods usually require the state to levy taxes on firms or individuals for funding. Consequently, the burden of justification is commonly placed on the provision of public goods. Even advocates supporting an extensive range of public goods acknowledge the need to justify their provision and offer justifications. However, alternative methods exist by which the state can ensure the provision of contingently public goods.

Regulation Prohibiting Exclusion: In cases where a non-rivalrous good already exists as a club good but is based on non-economic criteria like gender, the state can enact regulations prohibiting such forms of exclusion. This action enlarges access and transforms the good into a public one. For instance, consider a privately owned swimming pool that, due to certain criteria, functions as a club good. If the state introduces regulations preventing exclusion based on non-economic criteria and ensures a reasonable fee for universal access, the swimming pool becomes a public good. This approach does not necessitate state expenditure or taxation, although some might argue that issuing such regulations still constitutes a form of market interference.

Assignment of Property Rights: Providing certain contingent public goods may directly hinge on property rights' initial allocation and specification. Public lands, such as woods, lakes, and plains, inherently possess public good characteristics by being accessible to everyone for recreational purposes. The decision to assign private property rights to these lands predates the existence of a market, making it non-interfering with the market. Moreover, the public good character can be maintained for private goods if property rights are restricted to grant universal access, as exemplified by the "right to roam" tradition in the Nordic countries. Contingently, public goods highlight that decisions on public goods provision do not always amount to market interference; some pertain to the market's structural setup. While this point may be more theoretical, given the existing assignment of property rights in the real world, acknowledging the impact of initial property rights decisions on the availability of contingently public goods provides a principled justification for interference—particularly when accompanied by fair compensation where applicable.

Contingency Good and Access to Alternatives

The proposition to tackle economic inequalities by providing public goods assumes that these inequalities are primarily problematic due to resulting disparities in opportunity and access. Providing contingently public goods may not alter existing inequalities in private resource ownership. However, it can foster greater equality of opportunity and access by offering an alternative to market consumption. Inequalities in opportunity, access, and status may stem from economic disparities, but they are not strictly tied to them. Consider the example of a private country club, which typically imposes substantial membership fees, effectively excluding those who lack wealth. However, grounds for exclusion may extend beyond economic criteria. Historically, country clubs have imposed restrictions based on gender and race, aspects that may not directly correlate with financial means. Exclusion from such clubs may be more linked to gender or race than a lack of personal wealth.

Public goods possess the unique potential to address injustices in two additional ways. First, as freely available, public goods create a shared realm of experience and social interaction, constituting what Kallhoff terms "connectivity goods." These goods broaden access and serve as points of interaction, symbolizing a commitment to shared space and equality. This holds, especially for contingently public goods, whose provision as public goods is a more decisive expression of the commitment to equality. Second, more indirectly, the provision of public goods weakens the market's more exclusive modes of provision, diminishing the significance of club goods, particularly relevant for contingently public goods. The provision of contingently public goods can undermine the appeal of corresponding club goods, gradually reducing the power of exclusive private institutions and addressing inequalities in access and opportunity. For example, a public pool reduces the incentive for people to pay for access to private pools. This aspect is often overlooked but remains critical: the long-term strategy for addressing inequalities of access resulting from powerful private clubs may involve the provision of corresponding public goods as substitutes, gradually diminishing the appeal and power of exclusive private institutions and consequently reducing inequalities in access, opportunity, and perceived status.

How Contingently Public Goods Help to Address Injustice

Public goods—especially contingently—emerge as a natural but largely overlooked focal point for effectively addressing current injustices. Providing contingently public goods appears to be a preferable alternative to implement-ing a universal basic income (UBI) in certain scenarios. While the UBI has garnered support for reasons ranging from individuals' justified claims to their share of natural and social resources to its potential to combat gender and racial injustices, it consistently aims to redistribute private resources relative to the existing status quo. As noted earlier, compelling reasons exist to consider public goods a more economically efficient and politically feasible policy option. This holds, for instance, when non-rivalrous goods exist as club goods, allowing for universal access at minimal additional cost. Similarly, where adjusting private property rights can ensure public good provision, public goods may outperform a UBI.

However, the question remains: under what circumstances should the state address injustices through public goods, and when should redistributive measures be used? More broadly, what principles guide the types of public goods the state should provide? First, the normative question of whether a state should provide a particular public good depends on current social background conditions, necessitating specific arguments in favor of contin-gently public goods in individual cases. Second, the account does not prescribe how different considerations should be weighed, such as the importance of economic efficiency versus equal access or the value of solidarity. What is emphasized here is the potential of public goods to rectify existing injustices, particularly pronounced in the case of contingently public goods.

Free-Rider Problem

In the realm of social sciences, the free-rider problem represents a type of market failure that arises when individuals who derive benefits from resources, public goods, and common pool resources fail to pay adequately or do not pay at all. Public roads, libraries, and communal services are examples of goods susceptible to this problem. Free riders pose a challenge to common pool resources as they may overuse them without contributing through direct fees, tolls, or indirect taxes. Consequently, this may lead to underproduction, overuse, or degradation of the common pool resource. Despite people's natural inclination towards cooperation (prosocial behavior), free riders' presence has deteriorated cooperation, perpetuating the free-rider problem.

The free-rider problem revolves around limiting its negative consequences by clearly defining property rights and ensuring enforcement. This problem is particularly common with public goods, characterized by non-excludability and non-rivalrous consumption. Non-excludable goods mean non-payers cannot be prevented from utilizing or benefiting from the good. At the same time, non-rival consumption implies that one consumer's use does not diminish its availability for others. These characteristics reduce the incentive for consumers to contribute to a collective resource despite enjoying its benefits. A free rider can benefit from a non-excludable, non-rivalrous good, such as a government-provided road system, without contributing to its costs.

Another example is a coastal town building a lighthouse, where ships from various regions benefit without contributing to its expenses—a classic case of "free riding" on the navigation aid. Non-excludable and non-rivalrous consumption is also evident in crowd-watching fireworks. The number of viewers, whether they paid or not, does not affect the availability of the fireworks. In these examples, excluding non-payers is prohibitive, while collective consumption does not deplete the available resources.

While "free rider" originated in economic theories of public goods, similar concepts apply to collective bargaining, antitrust law, psychology, political science, and vaccines. For instance, team or community members might reduce their contributions or performance if they believe others in the group are free-riding. The economic free-rider problem extends to global politics, presenting challenges to international cooperation. States often face situations where certain actors benefit from collective goods or actions without contributing to the efforts or bearing the costs needed to achieve shared objectives. This imbalance hampers cooperative endeavors, especially in addressing global challenges like climate change, security, or humanitarian crises. In climate change discussions, countries with lower greenhouse gas emissions might benefit from global efforts without proportionally sharing the emission reduction costs, creating disparities and obstacles in negotiating effective international agreements. The manifestation of the economic free-rider problem in global politics underscores the complexities in fostering collective action and equitable burden-sharing among nations to address pressing global issues.

Incentives Contributing to the Free-Riding Problem

The underlying incentive contributing to the free-rider problem can be illustrated by applying the Prisoner's dilemma, particularly in contributing to a public good. Let us consider a scenario where two individuals decide to share the cost of contributing to a public service, like funding a police station, with society reaping the benefits. The Prisoner's dilemma sheds light on possible outcomes in this situation. If both parties contribute, they incur costs and benefit society. However, if one party chooses not to pay, hoping someone else will cover the cost, they become a free-rider, burdening the other contributor. Society gains no benefit if both parties opt to be free riders and neither pays, thus illustrating that the free-rider problem arises from individuals' willingness to let others bear the costs when they can receive the benefit at no personal expense. This tendency is further supported by the economic theory of rational choice, which posits that humans make choices to maximize their benefits. Consequently, when a service or resource is offered for free, individuals are less likely to contribute financially as they can enjoy the benefit without incurring any costs.

The Economic Efficiency Effect of Free-Riding

Free riding challenges economic efficiency when it results in the underproduction or overconsumption of a good. For instance, when individuals are asked to express how much they value a specific public good in terms of the money they would be willing to pay, they often underestimate their valuations. Goods susceptible to free-riding share common features: the inability to exclude non-payers, individual consumption that does not affect availability for others, and the resource that must be produced and maintained. Suppose a mechanism allows for the exclusion of non-payers. In that case, the good can be transformed into a club good (e.g., converting an overused public road into a toll road or turning a free public museum into a private, admission fee-charging museum).

Free riding becomes problematic when non-excludable goods are rivalrous, falling under common-pool resources. These goods face overconsumption when common property regimes are absent, with consumers benefiting without payment and one consumer's consumption imposing an opportunity cost on others. The 'Tragedy of the Commons' theory illustrates this: consumers seek to maximize their utility, relying on others to reduce their consumption. This often leads to overconsumption and potential depletion of the resource. In systems or services relying on external resources, free-riding occurs when the production of goods does not account for external costs, particularly in using ecosystem services.

A notable example is the global climate change initiatives. As climate change is a global concern without a unified global regime, the benefits of emission reductions in one country extend globally. However, some countries act self-interested, limiting their efforts and free-riding on others' work. This raises questions about fairness and ethics, especially when countries most vulnerable to the consequences of climate change emit fewer greenhouse gases and have fewer resources to contribute.

Achieving Pareto-Optimal Allocation: Economists commonly argue that achieving a Pareto-optimal allocation of resources for public goods is incompatible with individuals' fundamental incentives. Most scholars anticipate the free-rider problem as an ongoing public issue, viewing it as cyclical in capitalist economies, tied to shifting interests. In times of workplace stress and job insecurity, individuals invest less in the public sphere. However, when public needs rise, dissatisfied individuals become interested in collective action projects, reversing the momentum of free riding. Hirschman's model suggests that people are motivated by a leader's call to altruism, creating cycles of commitment and decline in collective action projects. However, critics like Milton Friedman find calls to altruism nonsensical and seek alternative solutions to address the free-rider problem.

Assurance Contracts

An assurance contract involves participants making a binding pledge to contribute to creating a public good contingent on reaching a predetermined quorum. If the quorum is not met, the good is not provided, and monetary contributions are refunded. In a dominant assurance contract, an entrepreneur initiates the contract and refunds the initial pledge and an additional sum if the quorum is not still needed to be reached. The entrepreneur profits by collecting a fee when the quorum is met, and the good is provided. In game-theoretic terms, pledging to build the public good is a dominant strategy, as it is optimal to pledge regardless of others' actions.

Coasian Solution

The Coasian solution, named after economist Ronald Coase, suggests that potential beneficiaries of a public good can negotiate to pool their resources and create it based on their self-interested willingness to pay. Coase argues that public goods can be produced without government intervention if transaction costs between potential beneficiaries are low. Coase later clarified that the "Coase theorem" explored a world with zero transaction costs but intended to understand the real world with positive transaction costs, corporations, legal systems, and government actions. A minor alternative, especially for information goods, involves producers withholding the release of a good (or part of it) until payment covers costs. This method, often called holding for ransom, relies on social norms to ensure the threshold is reached. A modern Coasian solution is Internet crowdfunding, where computer algorithms, legal contracts, and social pressure enforce rules. Platforms like Kickstarter authorize credit card purchases only when the funding goal is met, minimizing transaction costs for pooling resources.

Introducing an Exclusion Mechanism (Club Goods)

Another solution, especially for information goods, introduces exclusion mechanisms that turn public goods into club goods. Copyright and patent laws, for instance, aim to remove non-excludability by prohibiting reproduction but lead to private monopoly power. While addressing free rider problems, these laws create inefficiencies, encourage litigation, and may not be Pareto-optimal. Exclusion mechanisms can naturally lead to club goods if the costs are lower than the collaboration gains. James M. Buchanan argues that clubs can be an efficient alternative to government interventions. However, inefficiencies and inequities sometimes prompt potential club goods to be treated as public goods, with production financed by other mechanisms like government subsidies or volunteer associations. Such goods are known as social goods. Joseph Schumpeter's theory of "Schumpeterian creative destruction" suggests that excess profits from copyright or patent monopolies attract competitors, leading to technological innovations and the end of the monopoly. This theory's applicability to different public goods types remains controversial. Examples include Microsoft's practices predicting increased market shares for Linux and Apple. By extension, a nation can be seen as a "club" managed by the government, as studied in the theory of the state.

Non-Altruistic and Non-Altruistic Social Sanctions

Common Property Regimes

Drawing on game theory and experimental literature, addressing free-riding situations might not require state intervention. Instead, the focus could be on the impact of different social sanctions. Peer-to-peer punishment, where group members sanction those who do not contribute to a common pool resource by imposing costs on "free-riders," is an effective means to establish and maintain cooperation. Punishing free riders comes at a cost to the punisher, necessitating a system where punishers are rewarded for their actions. Unlike a prisoner's dilemma where communication is restricted, groups can form "common property regimes" to weigh the costs and benefits of rewarding individuals for sanctioning free riders. As long as the benefits of preserving the resource outweigh the communication and enforcement costs, members often compensate punishers. While not Pareto-optimal due to the additional cost of enforcement, it is often more economical than resource depletion. In cases where bargaining and enforcement costs approach zero, the setup becomes Coasian, moving toward the Pareto-optimal solution.

Both punishment and state regulation are less effective under imperfect information, where people cannot observe others' behavior. Common property regimes, established through bargaining, usually have more information about the managed resource than outsiders. This local knowledge advantage, combined with avoiding the principal-agent problem, often enables common property regimes to outperform regulations imposed by external technical experts. Optimal performance is typically achieved when people in common property regimes consult with governments and technical experts to decide on rules and designs, blending local and technical knowledge.

Altruistic Solutions - Social Norms

Psychologically, humans are perceived as free-riders when they consume benefits without contributing. This recognition is universal, but cultural differences exist in tolerance and dealing with free riders. Social norms play a significant role in privately and voluntarily providing public goods. Social sanctioning, in particular, is a widely recognized norm with a high degree of universality. Research on social sanctioning and its impact on the free-rider problem aims to explain the observed altruistic motivation in various societies. Free riding is often narrowly considered in terms of positive and negative externalities, neglecting the impact of social norms on actions and motivations related to altruism, which economic solutions and models often

27

underestimate. While non-altruistic social sanctions are evident when people establish common property regimes, individuals sometimes punish free-riders without expecting any reward. The precise nature of this motivation remains to be explored. There is an ongoing dispute over whether costly punishment can effectively explain cooperation. Recent research indicates that costly punishment is less impactful in real-world environments.

In examining social sanctions in the context of public goods, some research suggests that preferences between secret sanctions (untraceable sanctions between players) and standard sanctions (traceable sanctions with feedback between players in an otherwise identical environment) on free-riders do not significantly vary. Interestingly, certain individuals prefer to sanction others regardless of secrecy. Building on behavioral economics findings, other research reveals that donors are motivated by the fear of loss in a dilemmatic donation game. In this game, donors' deposits are only refunded if they consistently punish free-riding and non-commitment among other individuals. Pool punishment (everyone loses their deposit if one donor does not punish the free rider) provides more stable results than punishment without considering the group's consensus. Individual-to-individual peer punishment leads to less consistently applied social sanctions. While this research is experimental, its application in public policy decisions aiming to address free-rider problems in society could prove beneficial.

Potential Solutions to the Free Rider Problem

Taxes: Requiring all consumers to pay taxes ensures no free riders, as seen in the example of national defense costs in the United Kingdom. Taxes, paid by everyone, eliminate free riding, and benefits are enjoyed universally.

Privatization of Public Goods: Converting public goods into private ones, with a payment requirement for consumption, eliminates free riders.

Donation Solicitation: Effective for low-cost public goods, soliciting voluntary donations helps offset free riding. For instance, gardens or museums may seek donations, reducing the impact of free riders.

Review Questions

1. Why does the chapter argue that concerns about economic inequality should extend beyond income distribution?
2. How do contingently public goods address economic inequalities more efficiently than traditional redistribution methods?
3. What are the political advantages of providing public goods universally, especially in the case of contingently public goods?
4. Explain the two methods discussed in the chapter to ensure the provision of contingently public goods without relying on traditional taxation.
5. According to the text, How can contingently public goods foster greater equality of opportunity and access?
6. Discuss the economic efficiency effects of free-riding and how it can impact the provision of public goods.

Discussion Points

1. Ethical Considerations: What ethical considerations should be considered when implementing policies related to contingently public goods, especially considering potential limitations and challenges?
2. Balancing Market Forces: How can policies ensure the provision of contingently public goods without eliminating market forces, considering the potential drawbacks of subsidies and regulation?
3. Global Perspective: How might the concepts discussed in the chapter apply or differ in a global context, especially in addressing economic inequalities on an international scale?

CHAPTER THREE: FISCAL POLICY: ALLOCATION, DISTRIBUTION, AND STABILIZATION

Summary of Key Points

1. Distribution Function in Public Finance:

- Determining tax and transfer payment policies is crucial for adjusting wealth and income distribution.
- Factors like earnings abilities, inherited wealth, and market pricing influence income and wealth distribution.
- Measures like the Lorenz curve and Gini coefficient assess income distribution and inequality.

2. Optimal Distribution:

- Defining a fair distribution is crucial, given that market-determined disparities may not align with societal values.
- Modern welfare economics, while emphasizing efficiency, faces challenges in achieving equitable income distribution.
- Shifting focus from equality to poverty prevention and ensuring adequate lower-end incomes is essential.

3. Fiscal Instruments in Distribution Policy:

- Redistribution policies primarily rely on tax-transfer schemes, including progressive income taxation and subsidies.
- Efficiency costs associated with distribution policies necessitate a balance between conflicting objectives.
- Direct income taxes and transfers are considered less distorting mechanisms for achieving distribution goals.

4. The Stabilization Function:

- Fiscal policy aims to maintain high employment, price stability, and economic growth through monetary and fiscal policies.
- Economic uncertainties require strategic intervention to achieve full employment and price stability.
- Stabilization policies must navigate international challenges and adjust aggregate expenditures periodically.

5. Fiscal and Monetary Instruments of Stabilization Policy:

- The fiscal system immediately impacts demand, with deficits being expansionary and surpluses being restrictive.
- Monetary policy tools, such as reserve requirements and discount rates, control the money supply for short-term stability and long-term growth.
- The policy mix, combining fiscal and monetary measures, is essential for achieving multiple economic objectives.

6. The Coordination or Conflict of Functions in Fiscal Policy:

- Fiscal policy functions include allocation, distribution, and stabilization, with conflicts arising in their implementation.
- Conflicts may occur between allocation and distribution, allocation and stabilization, distribution and stabilization, and distribution and growth

objectives.

· Normative coordination in fiscal policy is an ideal standard, but practical conflicts often arise during implementation.

Distribution Function in Public Finance

Public finance's distribution function tackles the challenge of adjusting wealth and income distribution for fairness. In a market economy, disparities in income and wealth distribution are common. This function involves determining tax and transfer payment policies, making distribution contentious in public policy decisions. Several factors influence the distribution of income and wealth in the absence of policy measures aimed at adjustment. Initially, it depends on the distribution of factor endowments, such as varying earnings abilities and inherited wealth ownership. The competitive market's factor pricing process, which aligns factor returns with the value of the marginal product, further determines income distribution based on factor supplies and market prices. Economists use the Lorenz curve and other measures like the Gini coefficient to represent income distribution within a society and assess inequality.

However, the resulting distribution may not align with societal notions of fairness or justice, prompting a distinction between the economic principle of efficient factor use and the proposition that market forces should fix income distribution among families. While the former ensures resource efficiency, the latter may lead to an unacceptable distribution pattern, especially in capital income. Determinants of income and wealth distribution encompass factors' contribution to the production process, the market value of factors' product, natural endowments, inheritance, societal preferences, political preferences, tax policies, labor union policies, the labor market, individual abilities, education, globalization, gender, race, and culture.

Optimal Distribution: Defining a fair or just distribution state becomes crucial, considering that a market-determined distribution may not align with societal values. Modern welfare economics, emphasizing economic efficiency without much regard for distributional considerations, relies on the

Pareto optimality criterion. This criterion, stating that an economic change is efficient if someone gains without anyone else losing, has limitations when applied to redistribution measures that improve one's position at the expense of others. Achieving equity in income distribution faces challenges, such as comparing individual utility levels derived from income and the efficiency cost associated with redistribution policies. Despite these challenges, distributional considerations remain central to public policy discussions. The focus is shifting from relative income positions and overall equality to ensuring adequate income at the lower end, emphasizing poverty prevention and establishing tolerable cutoffs rather than imposing ceilings at the top.

Fiscal Instruments in Distribution Policy

The implementation of redistribution policies primarily relies on tax-transfer schemes, incorporating progressive income taxation for high-income households and subsidies for low-income households. Progressive income taxes fund public services, including redistribution efforts like public housing. Alternatively, redistribution may be achieved through taxes on goods primarily purchased by high-income consumers and subsidies for goods predominantly used by low-income consumers. When selecting among policy instruments, it is essential to consider potential "deadweight losses" or efficiency costs arising from interference with consumer or producer choices. While an income tax-transfer mechanism has the advantage of not significantly affecting specific consumption or production choices, it does introduce efficiency costs, particularly in the choice between income and leisure. Despite these efficiency costs, it remains a less distorting mechanism than more selective measures. Therefore, direct income taxes and transfers may fulfill the distribution branch's function.

Redistribution policies that incur efficiency costs do not inherently argue against their implementation. Instead, they suggest that any distributional change should be accomplished with minimal efficiency costs, necessitating a balance between conflicting policy objectives. Achieving efficiency in a broad sense requires considering both concerns. The following points are pertinent:

1. The market mechanism may not achieve the optimal distribution of re-sources because societal preferences may differ from market preferences.
2. Various factors, including societal culture and political preferences, must be considered when distributing societal resources.
3. Tax and income-transfer policies serve as primary tools for government distribution policies.

The distribution resulting from the market's pattern of factor endowments and factor services sales may not align with societal fairness, necessitating distributional adjustments through tax and transfer policies.

The Stabilization Function

Fiscal policy aims to maintain or achieve high employment, reasonable price stability, and appropriate economic growth, accounting for trade and balance of payments effects. The primary instruments of stabilization policy are monetary and fiscal policies, collectively known as compensatory finance, whose objectives are the following:

1. Comprehend the purpose of stabilization.
2. Understand the instruments of stabilization policy.
3. Grasp the concept of policy mix.
4. Explore effective ways to shape policy.

The Imperative of Stabilization: Achieving full employment and price stability is not an automatic outcome in a market economy; it necessitates strate-gic intervention through public policy. Without effective fiscal policy for stabilization, the economy may undergo substantial fluctuations, leading to prolonged periods of unemployment or inflation. Compounding the challenge, both unemployment and inflation may coexist. Acknowledging the need for public policy to address these uncertainties does not negate the possibility that poorly executed public policy might contribute to destabilization. The economy's overall employment and price levels hinge on aggregate demand relative to potential or capacity output at prevailing prices. Aggregate demand, determined by the spending decisions of numerous stakeholders, including consumers, corporate managers, financial investors, and unincorporated operators, depends on factors like past and present income, wealth position, credit availability, and expectations. In some periods, expenditures may fall short, hindering the guarantee of full employment of economic resources. Due to downward rigidity in wages, prices, and other factors, the automatic restoration of such employment needs to be improved. Expansionary measures are essential to boost aggregate demand in these situations. Conversely, during periods of high employment, excessive expenditures may lead to inflation, requiring restrictive measures to curtail demand. Deficient demand or inflationary conditions lack an automatic adjustment process to restore the economy to high employment and stability.

Complicating matters, economies are interconnected through trade and capital flows, making policies affecting domestic income and prices also impact a country's exports, imports, and balance of payments, influencing other nations' economic positions. Stabilization policy must navigate the intricate challenges of international policy coordination. While stabilization in the thirties and forties focused on achieving full employment within a given potential output, post-fifties developments shifted attention to potential output growth and inflation. Adjusting aggregate expenditures periodically is imperative to align demand with potential output growth, considering factors like population increase and productivity. Public policy may also seek to influence the growth rate of potential output, emphasizing the strategic importance of saving and investment incentives due to their impact on growth, particularly in capital formation. More recently, the primary focus has shifted to inflation. After reaching high employment levels in the mid-sixties, the challenge became restraining inflation without compromising the full-employment objective, as evident in the seventies, where policies had to combat inflation and unemployment simultaneously.

Fiscal and Monetary Instruments of Stabilization Policy

The fiscal system's presence has an immediate and inevitable impact on the level and structure of demand. Even if fiscal policy aims for neutrality, its effects on aggregate demand must be considered to ensure such neutrality. Additionally, changes in budget policy can actively influence or counteract shifts in demand.

Leverage Effects of Given Budget: Government expenditures boost total demand, while taxes reduce it. This implies that budgetary effects on demand are significant when expenditures are high and tax revenue is low. Deficits are expansionary, surpluses are restrictive, and even a balanced budget has an expansionary impact.

Changes in Budget Policy: Discretionary policy measures can be employed to alter aggregate demand. Government expenditures may be increased or tax rates reduced to expand demand, and vice versa for contraction. The policy challenge extends beyond the direction of change to selecting the appropriate type and magnitude based on the specific adjustments to consumption or investment in the private sector.

Built-in Responses: Adjustments in public expenditures or tax rates are utilized to influence overall demand, and changes in economic activity affect public expenditures and tax revenue. The fiscal system inherently possesses flexibility that adapts to economic changes, such as unemployment benefits and welfare variations during different economic conditions.

Monetary Instruments: While the market mechanism is adept at allocating resources among private goods, it needs to improve in regulating the money supply. Money, as Walter Bagehot noted, does not control itself. The central banking system must control the money supply, aligning it with short-term stability and long-term growth needs through monetary policy tools like reserve requirements, discount rates, open market policies, and selective credit controls.

Policy Mix: The combination of fiscal and monetary policy, known as the policy mix, is crucial to achieving multiple objectives. Monetary and fiscal measures complement each other, and using them in tandem can achieve more objectives than relying on a single policy instrument. A blend of easy money and a tight budget favor economic growth.

Fiscal and monetary policies are interconnected, with monetary policy having a special advantage in securing balance of payments adjustments due to its impact on international capital movements. Fiscal policy, on the other hand, is more effective in addressing domestic needs. Budgetary imbalances, either surplus or deficit, are essential fiscal policy tools that affect the structure of claims, including money and public debt. Fiscal and monetary policies interact and complement each other but share the same weakness. While effective in managing aggregate demand imbalances related to unemployment and inflation, these measures are less effective in addressing stagflation, where structural maladjustments in various markets underlie the issue. In summary, our exploration of the stabilization function has underscored the following points:

1. Full employment and price stability necessitate public policy guidance.
2. The fiscal system immediately influences demand levels and structures.
3. Monetary and fiscal measures, while differing in impact, can supplement each other through a policy mix.

Theoretically, budget policies can harmonize allocation, distribution, and stabilization objectives, but practical conflicts and distortions frequently arise.

The Coordination or Conflict of Functions in Fiscal Policy

After delving into the primary functions of the public sector in the economy—allocation, distribution, and stabilization—we must explore how these functions are coordinated or conflicted in the context of fiscal policy. It is crucial to differentiate between a normative perspective, where policies are ideally coordinated for the simultaneous achievement of objectives, and a descriptive one that reflects the practical complexities and conflicts encountered in actual policy implementation. The analysis of policy implementation should help to:

1. Understand the coordinated approach within a normatively conducted fiscal process.
2. Grasp how conflicts arise and are coordinated in the fiscal process.
3. Recognize that budget policies can be designed to accomplish allocation, distribution, and stabilization objectives without conflict.
4. Understand the distinctions between the public and private sectors, acknowledging their interactions in product and factor markets and in the income and expenditure flows of the economy.

Coordination of Fiscal Policy Objective

In analyzing public policy, economists emphasize that the number of policy tools must align with the number of policy targets to avoid conflicts. Given the three targets of allocation, distribution, and stabilization, three distinct policy instruments are needed. Think of these as separate sub-budgets or fiscal branches, each dedicated to its specific objective.

Distribution: Design a tax-transfer plan to achieve the desired adjustment in distribution based on the assumption that a full employment income level is achievable.

Allocation: Provide for social goods, financed by taxes in line with consumer evaluation, based on the assumption that the distribution branch achieved the "proper" income distribution, and the stabilization branch has secured full employment.

Balanced Budget: Provide necessary adjustments in aggregate demand based on the assumption that the distribution and allocation branches have fulfilled their tasks.

The three sub-budget plans are interdependent, requiring simultaneous determination. Once determined, administrative convenience prompts clearing the taxes, transfers, and net payments against each other. The resulting net transfers, taxes, and government purchases for allocation branch services form the combined or net budget, representing a composite of the three sub-budgets. The net budget may exhibit a deficit or surplus, depending on the stabilization branch's position. The progressivity or regressivity of the net payment system is only sometimes evident and may be influenced by both the distribution and allocation components.

Conflicts in Fiscal Policy Objectives

The distinction between the allocation, distribution, and stabilization aspects of fiscal policy not only aids in delineating distinct policy goals but also serves as a guide in navigating the complexities of fiscal politics. In the real-world scenario of budget planning, evaluating various policy objectives independently becomes challenging. Conflicts emerge as individual and group interests clash during implementation, often resulting in achieving one objective at the expense of another.

Allocation and Distribution: Redistribution is primarily accomplished through tax-transfer schemes but is also influenced by progressive tax finance for social goods provision. Two approaches are commonplace:

"Ability to Pay Approach": The tax burden is determined based on the taxpayer's ability to bear the sacrifice of income reduction, independent of the tax for social goods.

Linkage to Expenditure Levels: The degree of redistribution tends to vary with program levels, associating extensive provision for social goods with significant redistribution.

Allocation and Stabilization

During periods of unemployment, government expenditure increases are proposed for demand expansion, while during inflation, a case is made for expenditure reduction. Proper stabilizing adjustments are made through changes in taxes or transfers without affecting social goods provision at full-employment income levels. However, combining allocation and stabilization issues can lead to oversupply or undersupply of social goods and face opposition from different groups.

Distribution and Stabilization

During severe unemployment, calls are made for greater tax relief for lower-income groups, and in periods of inflation, arguments are presented for raising taxes on low-income groups. However, stabilization actions may interfere with redistribution, and biases may emerge, linking the two objectives unnecessarily. Stabilization adjustments can be made with distributionally neutral taxes.

Distribution and Growth

Higher growth objectives may demand increased saving and investment, potentially conflicting with redistribution objectives. Tax structure considerations should note that while high-income recipients have a higher propensity to save, conflicts may arise unless public investment is introduced or public saving is considered. The potential conflicts illustrate that the normative view of a seamlessly attuned sub-budget is not a realistic depiction of the fiscal process. Instead, it serves as a standard for measuring actual performance and evaluating the quality of existing fiscal institutions.

Interaction Between Private and Public Sectors

The preceding discussion underscores the distinctive roles of the public and private sectors. However, these sectors are interconnected and mutually influence the broader economic process.

Income and Expenditure Flows

Private Sector: Households earn income through factor market transactions (supplying labor), and this income is either spent or saved. Savings, in turn, fuel investment expenditure.

Product Market Transactions: Purchases of products in the product market contribute to firm receipts, which are then utilized for acquiring factor services.

Government Introduction: The government enters the scenario, purchasing factors and products alongside the private sector. Government revenue is derived from taxes and borrowing and makes transfer payments.

The government acts as a buyer in both factor and product markets, making its operations an integral part of the pricing system. Designing fiscal policies necessitates considering how the private sector will respond, as a tax imposed at one point may lead to shifts in burdens elsewhere.

Factor and Product Flows

Flow of Public Goods: The flow of public goods and services financed not through sales but through taxes or borrowing. Privately produced goods are sold to the government. Tax and expenditure policies influence aggregate demand and economic activity levels and contribute to maintaining economic stability, including high employment and inflation control. Despite their differing functions, the public and private sectors interact across product and factor markets and within the income and expenditure flows of the economy. In considering fiscal policies, whether conducted centrally or de-centrally, the diverse budgetary functions may be more or less suitable at different levels of governmental activity.

Public Revenue

The government's provision of goods and services requires resources, prompting a discussion of government revenue and methods of withdrawing resources from the private sector for public use. The four primary functions of fiscal policy are allocation, stabilization, distribution, and development. Taxation and government expenditure are fundamental tools employed in fulfilling these functions. As government activities expand in modern welfare states, the need for substantial public expenditure has risen. Adolph Wagner's "Law of Increase State Activities" highlights the regular increase in the activity of central and local governments among progressive societies.

Sources of Government Revenue: Public finance revolves around the diverse channels through which the state acquires income. These sources encompass taxes, commercial revenues from public enterprises, administrative revenues in fees and fines, and gifts and grants. Public revenue, or public income, can be defined in two ways—narrow and broader. In the narrow sense, it includes income from taxes, prices of goods and services supplied by public sector undertakings, and revenue from administrative activities such as fees and fines. In the broader sense, public revenue encompasses all government incomes during a specific period, including public borrowing and the issuance of new currency. Income from public enterprises is termed public receipts.

Public Receipts Clarification: Public receipts comprise all government income, including public borrowing and the issuance of new currency. Public revenue is thus a component of public receipts, as expressed by the formula:

Public Receipts = Public Revenue + Public Borrowing + Issue of New Currency

Money Creation: National governments can finance plans by instructing the Central Bank to print more money. Money creation is considered politically painless, especially when the economy faces substantial unemployment.

Borrowing involves exchanging purchasing power and acquiring money from the private sector for public use. Borrowing can be internal or external, with its significance dependent on the economic state—full employment or underemployment.

User Charges: Government charges for goods and services provided, known as user charges. These charges are tied to specific roles and differ from taxes, as they are linked directly to particular goods and services.

Commandeering of Resources: The government can finance public goods by commandeering physical resources from the private sector, such as labor and materials. However, this method could be more efficient and equitable.

Non-Tax Revenue: Non-tax revenue includes commercial revenue, administrative revenue (fees, fines, special assessment), gifts, grants, and others. Public enterprises earn commercial revenue through the sale of goods and services. Administrative revenue encompasses fees, fines, and special assessments for administrative functions. Gifts and grants refer to payments between governments for specific functions. Understanding these revenue sources provides insights into how governments fund their activities and deliver essential services to the public.

Review Questions

1. What are the key challenges in achieving fair income distribution in a market economy?
2. How do economists measure income distribution, and what role do tools like the Lorenz curve and Gini coefficient play?
3. What are the primary fiscal instruments used for distribution policy, and why is a balance between conflicting objectives necessary?
4. How does fiscal policy contribute to achieving full employment, price stability, and economic growth?
5. Explain the leverage effects of a given budget and how changes in budget policy can influence aggregate demand.
6. Why is the policy mix of fiscal and monetary measures considered essential for effective economic management?

Discussion Points

1. Discuss the ethical considerations and challenges in defining what constitutes a fair or just distribution of income and wealth in society.
2. Explore the potential conflicts that may arise between different fiscal policy objectives and the trade-offs involved in resolving them.
3. Analyze the role of international coordination in stabilization policy and the challenges associated with managing economic stability in interconnected global economies.

CHAPTER FOUR: FISCAL FEDERALISM: BALANCING REVENUE, EXPENDITURE, AND EQUITY

Summary of Key Points

1. Taxable Capacity:

- Modern states face increased public expenditure, transforming from police to welfare states.
- Taxation is a major revenue source impacting purchasing power and economic activities.
- Scholars like Dalton, Stamp, Shirras, and the Indian Taxation Enquiry Commission provide diverse perspectives on taxable capacity.

2. Determinants of Taxable Capacity:

- Various factors influence taxable capacity, including national income, population, standard of living, and political conditions.
- The discussion covers the impact of fiscal, monetary, and income policies, technological progress, and modernization on taxable capacity.

3. Equalization of Fiscal Position:

- Intergovernmental fiscal relations correct spillover benefits and ensure fiscal equalization.
- Approaches include matching grants, common minimum levels, and eliminating differences in service levels.
- Central responsibility for stabilization actions is crucial, but decentralized fiscal policy has limitations.

4. Benefit Spillovers:

- A mismatch between jurisdictions and benefit-tax cost areas leads to benefit spillovers.
- Factors include complexities of benefit areas, mobility of people and businesses, and historically given jurisdictions.
- Internalizing spillovers requires compensation mechanisms or boundary adjustments.

5. Fiscal Differentials and Distortions in Location:

- Fiscal coordination is essential to address distortions in location decisions due to fiscal advantages or disadvantages.
- Focus on equalizing tax costs and understanding net differentials to prevent hindrances to inefficient production.

6. Equity Advantages of Central Taxes:

- Central taxes help avoid distortions in location and promote equality.
- Progressive taxation is challenging at lower levels, and grants from the federal level impact progressivity.
- Balancing fiscal decentralization advantages and location decision distortions is essential.

Taxable Capacity

Recently, public expenditure has significantly increased, primarily due to the manifold expansion of government functions. Modern states have transformed from police to welfare states, necessitating substantial revenue to meet financial obligations. Taxation is the major revenue source, although its implementation impacts people's purchasing power and willingness to work, save, and invest. Therefore, considering the population's capacity to pay taxes is crucial when adjusting tax rates or introducing new taxes. Different scholars present various perspectives on taxable capacity:

1. Professor Dalton describes taxable capacity as a common but dim and confusing concept.
2. Josiah Stamp Defines it as the minimum amount citizens can pay without leading to a miserable existence or disrupting the economic organization.
3. Findlay Shirras: Views taxable capacity as the limit of squeezability, representing the surplus of production over the minimum consumption required.
4. Indian Taxation Enquiry Commission-1954: Refers to taxable capacity as the degree of taxation beyond which productive efforts and efficiency start to suffer.

Determinants of Taxable Capacity

Several factors influence taxable capacity, including:

1. National income and wealth
2. Size of population
3. Standard of living
4. Nature of public expenditure
5. The psychological attitude of the people
6. Stage of economic growth
7. Political conditions

8. Tax structure
9. Fiscal, monetary, and income policies
10. Favorable balance of trade
11. The inflow of foreign capital
12. Technological progress
13. Modernization of production patterns, etc.

This discussion on public revenue has covered the main sources of government revenue, the definition of taxable capacity, and the determinants shaping it.

Equalization of Fiscal Position: Intergovernmental fiscal relations, involving fiscal transactions among various government levels, exist for reasons such as correcting spillover benefits, subsidizing local public services, ensuring equalization in lower-level jurisdictions, moderating fiscal differentials, and addressing advantages of central government taxation. Central responsibility for stabilization actions is crucial due to trade leakages, monetary policy effectiveness, and access to national capital markets. While decentralized fiscal policy for stabilization is limited, central governments may influence lower-level fiscal behaviors for various reasons, including raising local public service levels and ensuring fiscal equalization. Different approaches to fiscal equalization include matching grants, common minimum levels, equalizing costs in terms of tax effort, and eliminating differences in service levels resulting from income or wealth disparities. These policies aim to equalize the provision of local social goods rather than redistributing individual income or general well-being.

Benefit Spillovers: One significant reason for coordinating adjustments among jurisdictions is the mismatch between existing jurisdictions and benefit-tax cost areas, leading to benefit spillovers. Several factors contribute to these spillovers:

Complexities of Benefit Areas: Benefit areas for different public services may have distinct spatial patterns, requiring overlapping jurisdictions for each service. Residents might be part of various "service clubs" with different scopes, adding complexity to the system. Administrative and political costs favor a more consolidated and simplified system, deviating from the equivalence principle between taxing and benefit areas.

Mobility of People and Businesses: The mobility of people and businesses introduces non-equivalence, where benefits from public expenditures in one jurisdiction can be transferred to another. For instance, educated individuals migrating out of a jurisdiction export the benefits of education expenditures. Suburban residents might consume services like police and fire protection in the city without contributing to decision-making or payment.

Historically Given Jurisdictions: Existing jurisdictions are often historically determined and not solely based on fiscal rationality. State or city boundaries may need to align more neatly with benefit limits, and adjustments are not easily made for fiscal reasons. Historical factors contribute to benefit and cost spillovers between jurisdictions.

To efficiently determine public service levels, spillovers must be internalized. Compensation mechanisms or boundary adjustments may be necessary to address undersupply issues of public goods. Countries have witnessed a trend towards creating special government agencies to handle functions with cross-boundary benefits, requiring intergovernmental cooperation or direct negotiations between jurisdictions. This issue parallels the discussion of benefit externalities from personal consumption, resembling the small-number case. If Jurisdiction A provides a service with spillover benefits to Jurisdiction B, negotiation and internalization efforts may be needed for efficient provision. While negotiation tends to lead to some internalization, achieving an entirely efficient solution is not guaranteed.

Fiscal Differentials and Distortions in Location

Fiscal coordination becomes crucial when fiscal advantages or disadvantages in specific jurisdictions distort location decisions for taxpayers, be they corporations or individuals. The preference for one jurisdiction over another arises due to differences in tax structures and the perceived benefits of public services. These differentials impact both product and factor flow, hindering efficient production. The focus is not solely on equalizing tax costs but on understanding the net differential or fiscal residue, whether the excess of benefits over costs or costs over benefits. While coordination is especially vital at the international level with large fiscal differentials, it also arises within a single country to a limited extent.

Equity Advantages of Central Taxes

Central taxes offer benefits not only in avoiding distortions in location but also in terms of promoting equality. The broader economy can serve as the tax base, allowing for a more comprehensive definition, especially with taxes like the corporation profits tax. Furthermore, the effective application of progressive taxation is challenging for lower-level jurisdictions, making it a function best suited for the federal level. As the overall tax system's burden distribution is a weighted average of federal, state, and local taxes, the progressivity depends on their respective revenue shares. Without grants, these shares are determined by each level of government's expenditures. The use of grants from the federal to the state and local levels involves revenue sharing, with the federal government transferring income tax revenue back to the state of origin. However, this transfer of taxing function to a higher level creates a dilemma, as each jurisdiction should ideally determine and pay for services limited to its benefits. If all taxes were based on benefits, these differentials and distortions in location decisions would be eliminated. This ideal scenario would only exist if "benefit taxation" meant setting taxes equal to total benefits rather than marginal benefits. The challenges of jurisdictional dilemmas must be addressed to strike a balance between the advantages of fiscal decentralization and the resulting distortions in location decisions.

Fiscal Federalism

A federation, a political association where two or more states form a political unity with a common government while retaining internal autonomy, brings attention to decentralized fiscal systems or fiscal federalism. This focus has grown due to the extension of the theory of social goods to the concerns of state and local governments. Developments in fiscal structures across many countries, including imbalances in resource distribution and needs among jurisdictions, have prompted a reevaluation of the fiscal roles performed by different government levels and their interrelations. This unit delves into the theoretical aspects of fiscal federalism, providing insights into the Nigerian context.

Fiscal federalism, also known as fiscal decentralization or multilevel finance, occurs when different layers of government influence the same individuals, especially in government expenditure and revenue. Many countries, including Nigeria, South Africa, Germany, France, Brazil, Ethiopia, Canada, and the USA, practice multilevel finance. In a federation, legislative, executive, and financial powers are divided between the central and state governments. The following key principles are required for the effective functioning of a federation:

1. Principle of Independence and Responsibility: Governments should have independent financial resources and be responsible for raising funds to meet their obligations. Financial independence and responsibility are fundamental for successful fiscal federalism. Federal and state governments should have the freedom to operate financially within their spheres, ensuring they can fulfill their activities without constraints. Taxing autonomy and spending autonomy should go hand in hand.

2. Principle of Adequacy and Elasticity: Resources of the federal and local governments should be adequate to fulfill their respective obligations. Expanding resources in response to needs must be flexible, especially during internal and external crises.

3. Administrative Economy and Efficiency: Administrative costs should be minimized, and measures should be in place to prevent tax evasion. Proper resource allocation between the central and state governments enhances administrative efficiency.

4. Principle of Uniformity and Equity: Resources should be distributed without discrimination among different units in a federation. Contributions to federal taxes should align with the economic capacity of each state,

promoting equity in taxation.

5. Principle of Accountability: Governments in a federation should be accountable to their respective legislatures for spending and revenue decisions.

6. Principle of Fiscal Access: Federal and state governments should be free to tap new revenue sources within their prescribed areas to meet growing financial needs.

7. Principle of Transfer of Resources: Provisions should allow the transfer of resources from one state to another, promoting equitable resource allocation.

8. Principle of Federal Supervision: Federal government supervision ensures that state governments adhere to rules and regulations regarding taxation and expenditure.

9. Principle of Integration and Coordination: The financial system of a federation should be well-integrated and coordinated for efficient functioning.

10. Social Principle of Federal Finance: Fiscal equity demands equal net fiscal benefits for individuals in similar economic circumstances across the nation.

Fiscal equity can be achieved by equalizing transfers and imposing basic minimum national standards for certain public goods.

Types of Fiscal Imbalances

In a federal nation, fiscal imbalances manifest in two forms: vertical fiscal imbalance and horizontal fiscal imbalance.

Vertical Fiscal Imbalance: In an ideal federation, there is a balance between expenditure responsibilities and taxing powers at each level of government. Vertical fiscal imbalance occurs when there is a disparity between expenditures and revenues at different government levels. This imbalance arises when one level of government has more financial resources than needed while another needs more resources for its functions. Intergovernmental grants often address this imbalance, complementing the allocation of taxing powers.

Horizontal Fiscal Imbalance: Horizontal fiscal imbalance denotes economic inequalities among states, requiring some states to set higher overall tax levels than others to achieve equal standards in public expenditure. This imbalance results from differences in economic factors such as area, climate, topography, soil, mineral resources, and factor endowments. It does not provide a rationale for intergovernmental transfers and is not externally imposed on state fiscal management.

Merits and Consequences of Fiscal Federalism

Merits

1. Alignment with Society Preferences: Fiscal federalism permits the allocation of resources based on people's preferences for public goods.
2. Effective Collective Decision-Making: Decentralization leads to smaller groups making collective decisions, fostering a more direct relationship between benefits and costs.
3. Experimentation and Innovation: Federating units can experiment with different approaches, leading to innovation and the adoption of successful techniques. Diseconomies of scale are avoided through this competitive experimentation.
4. Optimal Allocation of Functions: Optimal allocation considers the geographical range of spillover effects and economies of scale in production. The government provides goods and services benefiting the entire nation, while local and state governments handle geographically divisible activities.

Consequences of Fiscal Fragmentation

1. Challenges in Attaining Optimal Tax Structure: Fiscal fragmentation makes achieving an optimal tax structure challenging, as simultaneous tax adjustment by all levels of government is difficult.

2. Reduction in Tax Capacity: Fragmented tax structures reduce the overall tax capacity of lower levels of government, impacting their ability to finance activities effectively. Fear of state competition may result in a reluctance to raise taxes, affecting the services provided.

3. Unequal Fiscal Capacity: Fragmentation leads to unequal fiscal strength due to differences in population and income among states. Richer states may disproportionately carry services, while poorer states may face challenges maintaining service levels.

4. Administrative and Compliance Challenges: Duplication of activities in a fragmented fiscal system complicates administration and compliance, posing challenges for effective governance.

Fiscal Federalism: The Nigerian Case

Nigeria's public finance has undergone significant changes since 1900, marked by key historical events. The merger of the colony of Lagos with the protectorate of Southern Nigeria in 1906 laid the foundation for subsequent developments. The artificial amalgamation of Northern and Southern Nigeria in 1914 by Sir Lord Lugard further shaped the fiscal landscape. Notably, before 1914, the South consistently recorded budget surpluses, while the North faced persistent deficits, often covered by the imperial government. During the initial twelve years (1914–1926) following amalgamation, limited centralization was observed, with distinct financial treatments for the North and South. However, from 1926 onward, complete centralization occurred, erasing distinctions between the two regions in the Nigerian budget.

The protectorate of Southern Nigeria was later divided into the Western and Eastern regions in 1939. From 1948 to independence in 1960, there was a degree of fiscal decentralization, albeit limited, in alignment with the pre-1926 practices. Native authorities were involved in tax collection during this period, establishing a parallel system of federal and native authorities collecting taxes. Constitutional developments in 1946 prompted a focus on fiscal federalism, leading to the establishment of the Philipson Fiscal Commission. This commission addressed fiscal responsibilities assigned to regional governments by the Richard constitution. Appointed in June 1946, Sir Philipson extensively examined revenue allocation schemes. The commission recommended three principles: derivation, population, and even progress (balanced development).

Derivation: This principle suggests allocating revenue to each region based on its contribution to centrally collected revenue. The aim was to instill fiscal discipline, align expenditure with revenue, and anticipate increased fiscal autonomy for regional governments. Critics argued that accurate determination of goods consumption was challenging due to the early stage of development, limited capacity for precise calculations, and the use of broad estimates, fostering regional antagonism.

Population: In the 1970s, the principles of equality of states and population gained prominence in revenue allocation. Population, albeit crudely used, aimed to link economic development with human capital and research. Challenges arose in achieving a complete population census for accurate revenue allocation.

Even Progress: Balanced regional development was recommended to prevent any state from lagging in the country's development. Additional principles like landmass (10 percent) and vertical allocation for different levels of government have also influenced revenue allocation. The vertical allocation formula has evolved, with the federal government consistently controlling a significant portion (around 70 percent) of total revenue. This high fiscal centralization often triggers intergovernmental fiscal conflicts and tensions when addressing revenue allocation among various levels of government in Nigeria.

Budgetary Process

The budgetary process typically involves two main sections: revenue and expenditure. The revenue section encompasses various government income sources, such as taxes, fees, grants, and borrowing. For instance, the U.S. federal budget incorporates revenue streams from individual and corporate taxes, social security contributions, and other avenues. On the other hand, the expenditure section outlines government spending across sectors like education, healthcare, defense, and infrastructure. A state budget might allocate funds for public education, covering aspects like teacher salaries, facilities, and educational programs. Governments project whether they will have a surplus (more revenue than expenditure) or a deficit (more expenditure than revenue) for the fiscal period, influencing fiscal policy decisions.

Some budgets distinguish between operational expenditures and capital expenditures. Capital budgets focus on long-term investments, such as building infrastructure. For example, a city might allocate funds in its capital budget to construct a new bridge. Budget proposals are prepared by government agencies, outlining their financial needs and objectives. This phase involves consultations and negotiations to align priorities with overall government goals. The proposed budget undergoes scrutiny by legislative bodies, involving debates, amendments, and approvals. Public input may be solicited through hearings, ensuring a democratic and transparent process. After approval, funds are allocated to different departments and agencies, and the government begins implementing the budget. Expenditures are monitored to ensure alignment with the approved plan. Audits are conducted to assess how well the budget was executed, providing insights into spending efficiency and effectiveness, which inform future budgetary decisions.

Fiscal Year and Budgeting Periods

Countries like the United States and Canada follow a calendar fiscal year from January 1 to December 31, simplifying reporting. Others, like the United Kingdom and India, use a financial year starting on April 1 and ending on March

31 of the following calendar year, aligning with agricultural and economic cycles. Some entities adopt hybrid fiscal years based on industry or specific needs. The choice of fiscal year affects the timing of budget preparation and execution. Understanding the components of a government budget, the budgetary cycle, and fiscal year variations is crucial for effective fiscal planning. Real-world examples illustrate the complexities and considerations in shaping budgets to meet diverse economic and industrial needs. Fiscal years may align with seasons relevant to specific economic activities. For instance, in agriculture-dependent economies, a fiscal year starting after the harvest season can better accommodate budgetary needs. Variations in fiscal year structures can complicate international comparisons of economic indicators. Efforts like those in the European Union aim to standardize reporting practices.

Examples

1. Example 1 - United States Federal Budget: The U.S. federal budget includes revenues from income taxes, corporate taxes, and spending on defense, healthcare (Medicare and Medicaid), and social security. The President's budget proposal undergoes review and approval by Congress. The fiscal year runs from October 1 to September 30, shaping government activities and economic policies.

2. Example 2 - United Kingdom Government Budget: The U.K. budget includes revenues from income taxes, value-added tax (VAT), and expenditures on education, defense, and public services. The U.K. follows an April-March fiscal year. The Chancellor of the Exchequer presents the budget to Parliament, guiding government spending for the fiscal year.

3. Case - India's Financial Year Change (2016): India shifted its fiscal year from April-March to July-June to align better with the monsoon season and improve budgetary planning for agricultural activities, aiming to enhance economic efficiency.

Review Questions

1. What are the key perspectives on taxable capacity presented by scholars like Dalton, Stamp, Shirras, and the Indian Taxation Enquiry Commission?

2. Discuss the factors influencing taxable capacity and their implications for adjusting tax rates.

3. How do benefit spillovers contribute to the complexities of fiscal coordination among jurisdictions?

4. Explain the role of central taxes in promoting equality and the challenges associated with progressive taxation at lower levels.

5. What are the consequences of fiscal fragmentation, and how does it impact the overall tax capacity of lower levels of government?

6. Describe the key principles required for the effective functioning of fiscal federalism, using examples to illustrate their application.

Discussion Points

1. Explore the trade-offs between the advantages of fiscal decentralization and the challenges arising from distortions in location decisions.

2. Discuss the role of historical factors in contributing to benefit and cost spillovers between jurisdictions and their implications for fiscal coordination.

3. Analyze a specific country's current fiscal federalism scenario, considering its adherence to the key principles and addressing any existing challenges.

CHAPTER FIVE: THE ROLE OF BUDGETS, DEBT, AND TAXATION IN ECONOMIC DEVELOPMENT

Summary of Key Points

1. Origins and Significance of Budget: The term "budget" originates from the French word "bougette," reflecting a document presented by the government detailing revenue and expenditure estimates for legislative approval. It encompasses financial actions from the previous year, current-year estimates, and future projections.

2. Features of Budget: The budget is a sanctioned, periodic (usually annual) statement prescribing revenue collection and Expenditure. It operates on a cash basis, adheres to the lapse rule, and emphasizes realistic estimation. Budgets are prepared on a departmental basis.

3. Objectives of a Budget: The budget serves multiple objectives, including resource reallocation, redistribution, and stabilization. It acts as a tool of government policy, ensuring financial and legal accountability, and is the basis of public welfare. Additionally, it estimates income and Expenditure, functioning as an instrument of fiscal policy.

4. Components of a Budget: Governments categorize budgets into revenue and capital budgets. The revenue budget deals with current financial transactions, while the capital budget focuses on capital receipts and payments involving borrowed funds for projects like construction.

5. Types of Budgets: Budgets are balanced (revenue equals Expenditure) or unbalanced (surplus or Deficit). Various deficit types include budgetary, revenue, and fiscal deficits, each reflecting different aspects of financial management.

6. Burden Transfer and Intergenerational Equity: The text explores the concept of burden transfer through debt financing and its implications for intergenerational equity. It delves into how debt burden affects future generations and examines the dynamics of burden transfer through diminished capital formation.

Budget

The term "budget" originates in the French word "bougette," signifying a leather bag or purse. In governmental contexts, a budget is commonly perceived as a document presented by the government containing estimates of proposed expenditures for a given period and the suggested means of financing them, subject to legislative approval. According to most countries' constitutions, governments must present an annual financial statement in parliament, showcasing revenue and expenditure estimates—commonly known as the annual financial statement or budget. Therefore, a government budget is a comprehensive schedule detailing all expected revenues and planned expenditures for the upcoming year. The budget incorporates:

1. Financial actions from the previous year.
2. Budget and revised estimates for the current year.
3. Budget estimates for the following year.

For instance, the budget for 2013-14 would encompass actual estimates from 2011-12, budget estimates and revised estimates for 2012-13, and budget estimates for 2013-14. The President typically presents the budget in the parliament, while state governments follow suit in their respective state legislatures in countries with a federal system of government.

Features of Budget

1. It is a statement of expected revenue and proposed Expenditure.
2. Some authority sanctions it.
3. It is periodic, generally annual.
4. It prescribes how revenue is collected, and Expenditures are incurred.
5. Budgets are prepared on a cash basis.
6. Rule of lapse: Unutilized funds within the year lapse at the end of the financial year.
7. Realistic Estimation.
8. Estimates on a Departmental Basis.

Objectives of a Budget

A budget is a vital tool in financial administration and an effective means of enforcing fiscal policies. The main objectives include:

1. Reallocation of resources.
2. Re-distribution of resources.
3. Stabilization of resources.
4. Providing information to the public about relevant governments' past, present, and future activities, plans, and programs.
5. Serving as a tool of government policy.
6. Estimation of income and Expenditure.
7. An instrument of fiscal policy.
8. Basis of public welfare.
9. Ensuring financial and legal accountability.

Components of a Budget

The government budget is categorized into revenue and capital budgets. The revenue budget pertains to the government's current financial transactions of a recurring nature. It includes revenue receipts and expenditures met from these revenues. On the other hand, the capital budget estimates capital receipts and payments over the fiscal year, focusing on increasing concrete assets or reducing recurring liabilities. The capital budget comprises receipts and expenditures and deals with borrowed funds, such as construction projects.

Types of Budgets

Budgets are categorized into balanced and unbalanced budgets based on the equilibrium between revenue and Expenditure.

Balanced Budget: A balanced budget is achieved when revenue matches Expenditure over a given period (Revenue = Expenditure).

Unbalanced Budget: Budget imbalances can result from excessive Expenditure over income or surplus income over Expenditure. In other words, budgets can be either in surplus or Deficit. A surplus budget occurs when public revenue exceeds outlay (R > E). Conversely, a deficit budget indicates that Expenditure surpasses revenue (R < E). Various types of deficits are associated with different receipts and expenditures, such as:

Budgetary Deficit: This Deficit reflects the difference between total receipts and government expenditures. It is typically financed by issuing 91-day treasury bills and depleting government cash balances with treasuries and central banks. The formula for budgetary Deficit is Total Revenue minus Total Expenditure.

Revenue Deficit: The excess of revenue expenditure over revenue receipts. Revenue Deficit = Revenue Receipts - Revenue Expenditure.

Fiscal Deficit: It represents the excess of total budget expenditures over total budget revenue, excluding borrowings. Fiscal Deficit equals the budgetary Deficit plus borrowings and other liabilities. The gross fiscal Deficit is the difference between total expenditure and revenue receipts, including non-debt capital receipts.

Mathematically, Fiscal Deficit = Total Expenditure - (Revenue Receipts + Non-debt Capital Receipts).

Net Fiscal Deficit = Gross Fiscal Deficit - Net loans and advances.

Fiscal Deficit measures the government's borrowing dependence to meet its budget expenditures. Consequences of fiscal Deficit include:

1. Accumulation of Public Debt.
2. Increase in the Burden of Interest Payments.
3. Generation of Inflationary Pressure.
4. Adverse Effects on Developmental Expenditure.

Monetized Deficit: It signifies the sum of the net increase in holdings of central bank treasury bills and its contributions to the government's market borrowings, resulting in an increase in high-powered or reserve money in the economy.

Debt Burden and Intergeneration Equity

Examining another aspect of the debt issue, it is argued that debt finance burdens future generations, both as a critique of borrowing and as an argument for securing intergenerational equity. The debate on debt burden revolves around concerns that deficit finance creates an obligation for future generations to bear the cost of services currently enjoyed. Opponents argue that the burden of all public expenditures ultimately falls on taxpayers, with loan finance deferring tax payments to when the debt is paid off. The opposing argument contends that interest payments impose no net burden on future generations since, assuming domestic debt, future generations will include taxpayers and interest recipients. However, this argument overlooks the frictional effects of taxation, where the severity of such effects may rise with increasing overall taxation. The proposition "we owe it to ourselves" is challenged by considering taxation's potential excess burden and deadweight losses. While debt accumulation during wars might lead to fiscal breakdown and debt repudiation in the postwar period, as long as the debt does not grow faster than GNP, the debt-GNP ratio remains stable. The severity of fiscal effects depends on factors like taxation ratios, and it is crucial to consider potential tax disincentives arising from increasing debt-GNP ratios.

Transfer of Burden Through Diminished Capital Formation

An essential facet of the burden issue is not merely the debt itself but the repercussions of loan and tax financing on growth and the legacy of capital bequeathed to successive generations. Returning to the framework of a "classical" system where investment aligns with saving at full employment, a unit of tax and loan finance reduces private expenditures by one unit. However, tax finance tends to impact private consumption, while loan finance leans towards affecting investment. For a constant set of public expenditures, substituting loans for tax finance diminishes the economic growth rate. This translates to a reduced endowment and lower income for future generations. The vehicle for this burden transfer is the contraction of endowment or net worth.

This burden transfer mechanism operates even when resource withdrawal from private use coincides with public Expenditure. In a narrower context, the generation releasing these resources bears the immediate cost. However, whether the resource withdrawal is from consumption or capital formation matters. In the former case, Generation 1, financing the Expenditure, bears the burden by reducing private consumption. In the latter case, it makes no such sacrifice but diminishes the future income and potential consumption of Generation 2. In transferring funds to the government, burden transfer occurs when Generation 1 responds by diminishing its capital formation in the private sector.

The argument that loan finance results in burden transfer while tax finance does not is rooted in the assumption that the former tends to impact capital formation while the latter does not. However, external loans input fresh resources without affecting aggregate consumption. Hence, the justification of tax finance over loan finance may not apply, especially when a low-interest external loan is involved. Thus, the government's ability to choose between loan and tax finance depends on which financing mix lowers aggregate demand. Under more realistic assumptions, tax finance may be more deflationary, resulting in a sharper reduction in private expenditures relative to loan financing. In such a system, the combination of tax and loan finance must be calibrated to achieve the desired level of aggregate demand, not just to secure an allocation of private resources between consumption and investment aligned with intergenerational considerations.

Burden Transfer with External Debt

As mentioned above, the mechanism of burden transfer through foreign borrowing differs in several aspects. Unlike domestic borrowing, there is no need for Generation 1 to curtail expenditures. Consumption and capital formation in the private sector can remain intact as additional resources needed for public outlay are sourced abroad. Loan finance now burdens Generation 2 not by leaving it with a diminished capital endowment at home but by imposing an obligation to service the foreign debt, which can, be shifted or carried over to Generation 3 with proper negotiations. The weight of external debt on a country is less severe than on firms and individuals. Taxes are paid to finance interest to foreigners instead of domestic debt holders. Generation 2 no longer owes the debt to itself. The foreign debt burden replaces the loss of capital income that Generation 2 would have suffered with domestic loan finance and a subsequent reduction in capital formation.

Comparing Taxation, Domestic Borrowing, and Foreign Borrowing

Assuming taxation impacts consumption and domestic borrowing influences capital formation, debt burdens the present generation, while domestic and foreign borrowing burdens the future. Although domestic and foreign borrowing share similarities in burdening the future, the choice between them may be open. It hinges on the cost of borrowing domestically and abroad. If the costs are equal, the burden on Generation 2 will be the same in each case. However, foreign borrowing may be preferable if domestic returns are higher and vice versa if domestic returns are lower.

Burden Transfer with Generational Overlap

When examining burden transfer between generations without overlapping lifespans, diminished private capital formation emerges as the primary mechanism, excluding foreign borrowing. However, reduced private capital formation is not a prerequisite when two generations overlap. If Generation 1 spans from year 1 to year 50, and Generation 2 from years 25 to 75, and all taxes come from consumption, it becomes feasible for Generation 1 to pay taxes in year 1 to sustain a government building's cost with a 50-year life. In return, taxes can be collected from Generation 2 in years 25 to 50, refunding Generation 1 and causing a shift in private consumption from Generation 2 to Generation 1. In this scenario, Generation 1, while initially bearing the entire burden, can transfer part of it to Generation 2. To reassure Generation 1, promises of repayment in the form of bonds may be given, redeemable later from taxes imposed on Generation 2.

This transfer among overlapping generations functions even without affecting capital formation in the private sector. As an alternative, Generation 1 may choose to make a present to Generation 2, assuming the entire burden without expecting repayment. This mirrors the mechanism seen when old-age retirement pensions were introduced and benefits were granted to the aged without requiring contributions.

Borrowing by State and Local Governments

The challenge of ensuring intergenerational equity is particularly pronounced at the state and local levels, where a substantial portion of public investment is executed and funded. Consider a township constructing a school building with a service life of thirty years. The project demands a significant, one-time surge in the township's overall Expenditure. If tax financing were employed, a temporary increase in the tax rate would be necessary, potentially unsettling for taxpayers who prefer a stable tax rate. More importantly, burdening only those paying taxes in a specific year would be unjust since the facility's utility spans thirty years. To address this, benefit taxation is applied, distributing the burden among successive "generations" benefiting from the service.

To achieve this, the initial cost is covered by borrowing externally. In subsequent years, future generations, reaping the benefits, are taxed annually based on their current benefit share. During this process, the debt is amortized and repaid when the facility is fully utilized. This method ensures intergenerational equity, with each generation bearing the cost of its benefit share. A township financing its school building through borrowing and gradual repayment thus establishes an equitable distribution of burdens across age groups and changing resident populations due to migration.

Burden Transfer in Development Finance

The burden above transfer mechanism has limitations when applied to development finance and economic growth. While it effectively spreads public investment costs, it is unsuitable for a development program. The challenge becomes more pronounced when considering a steady annual investment stream with a constant population. Current tax finance aligns with the present flow of benefits, assuming a disregard for the position of the discriminated first generation and the future benefits reaped by subsequent generations. The fundamental issue arises when public capital formation is loan-financed, offsetting a decline in private capital formation. This renders the mechanism ineffective for development programs. However, this limitation does not apply to foreign borrowing.

Justification for Burden Transfer

In justifying burden transfer, the principle that public services should be financed based on benefit taxation is paramount. Ensuring each generation pays for its received benefits aligns with intergenerational equity. For public capital outlays with future benefits, loan finance, and burden transfers become necessary for intergenerational equity. Assuming tax finance affects consumption, while loan finance influences capital formation, the combination of tax finance for current needs and loan finance for capital outlays adheres to intergenerational equity. This rationale supports using a capital budget for development finance, particularly in local finance and foreign borrowing. It also justifies relying on loan finance for wartime costs. From the exploration of debt burden and intergenerational equity, key observations include:

1. Debt management focuses on refunding maturing debt rather than its absolute level.
2. The public debt becomes part of the economy's claim structure, requiring service costs depending on the interest payments to GNP ratio.
3. Without generational overlap, burden transfer manifests as reduced capital formation.
4. Loan finance, falling more on investment, and tax finance, more on consumption, make loan finance a means of transferring a burden to future generations.
5. Foreign borrowing facilitates financing public programs without burdening the present generation, which is crucial for development finance.
6. Burden transfer aligns with intergenerational equity when public outlays lead to future benefits.

Development Finance

Economic development prerequisites include sustained economic growth, increased capital formation, and technological progress. Public finances, both on the tax and expenditure fronts, play a crucial role in economic development, especially in low-income countries like Nigeria. Capital formation, including physical and human capital investment, is fundamental to economic development. Early-stage development emphasizes public sector investment, establishing the framework for subsequent private investment. Mobilizing unused resources or securing additional resources from abroad becomes essential. Taxation is pivotal in providing savings incentives and disincentives to luxury consumption. Government budgeting becomes a key development finance source, focusing on public sector savings and capital formation.

In summary, while voluntary private saving is vital, early-stage development often relies on the government budget as a primary source of finance. Achieving economic development involves a mix of public and private investment, with taxation as a tool to incentivize savings and guide resource allocation. Public sector savings, generated through a surplus in the current budget, can fuel capital formation in the public and private sectors. The challenge lies in maintaining fiscal discipline to ensure that resources are channeled effectively for development purposes.

Technology, Enterprise, and Efficiency

Enhanced technology is pivotal in the developmental journey, impacting sectors like manufacturing and agriculture. The noteworthy surge in agricultural productivity across several developing nations in the past decade underscores the advantages of upgraded technology. Foreign private investment, a key contributor, brings improved technologies. However, adapting these technologies to the specific conditions and resources of less developed countries (LDCs) is crucial. Tax provisions can be tailored to incentivize the adoption of advanced techniques. The presence of business enterprises is essential for

69

a robust private sector, and the tax structure can be strategically designed to foster productive investments. Efficient resource utilization is critical in resource-scarce LDCs, which involves meticulous government expenditure evaluation, and a development plan circumvents wasteful bottlenecks during the developmental process.

Social and Political Factors

Economic development grapples with intractable issues related to social attitudes and organizations that necessitate modification for progress. Simultaneously, political stability is imperative for individual initiative, successful implementation of development plans, and essential economic transformation. Achieving widespread benefits from development is crucial, requiring the elimination of income inequality prevalent in many LDCs. While certain redistributive measures, like land reform, may not harm output levels and could be beneficial, conflicts may arise between income distribution policies and the objective of boosting saving and investment. Balancing public saving through increased taxation against private incentives for investment becomes a delicate trade-off.

Foreign Exchange

Foreign trade plays a pivotal role in many less developed economies, providing opportunities for specialization, economies of scale, and the exercise of comparative advantage. Foreign exchange earnings facilitate the purchase of crucial products, such as machinery and equipment, for which domestic technology may be lacking. Exports contribute to development by creating an expanding market, fostering "linkage" investments, and forming an "export-led" nexus. Public policy needs to address resource allocation between consumption and investment and domestic and traded products. The tax structure is instrumental in influencing the allocation process outlined in the development plan.

Balance and Bottlenecks

In the course of economic development, bottlenecks or growth limitations may emerge. Initially, the rate of internal saving may be the constraining factor, followed by the absorptive capacity of the economy to make productive investments. The development process may eventually strain the balance of payments, surpassing the capacity to earn foreign exchange for imports through exports. A well-conceived development plan should aim for balanced growth, with tax policy, in particular, employed to encourage capital inflow and influence the balance between imports and exports.

Role of Fiscal System

The fiscal system plays a multifaceted role in economic development. The level of taxation impacts public saving and, consequently, the resources available for capital formation. Both the level and structure of taxation influence private saving. Public investment, particularly in infrastructure, is crucial. Tax incentives and penalties can be strategically designed to enhance resource utilization efficiency. The distribution of tax burdens and expenditure benefits influences the equitable distribution of economic development benefits. The tax treatment of foreign investment affects capital inflow, reinvestment rates, and the taxation pattern relative to domestic products, influencing the foreign trade balance.

Review Questions

1. What key features distinguish a budget as a financial document in governmental contexts?
2. Explain the significance of the rule of lapse in budgetary practices.
3. Differentiate between revenue and capital budgets, highlighting their respective components.
4. How does a balanced budget differ from an unbalanced budget, and what

are the potential consequences of each?

5. Please elaborate on the types of deficits associated with government finances and their implications.

6. Discuss the arguments for and against burden transfer through debt finance, particularly intergenerational equity.

Discussion Points

1. How can a government balance the objectives of burden transfer for inter-generational equity while ensuring sustainable economic development?

2. How might the principles of benefit taxation be applied to different types of government expenditures to achieve intergenerational equity?

3. Evaluate the role of foreign borrowing in facilitating public programs without burdening the present generation, especially in economic development.

CHAPTER SIX: FISCAL STABILITY, GROWTH, AND RESOURCE ALLOCATION

Summary of Key Points

1. Fully Employed Economy and Domestic Savings Ratio:

   - Fiscal policy fosters stability and growth in less developed countries (LDCs), especially in a fully employed economy.
   - Understanding fiscal policy through this lens helps explain its impact on growing the domestic savings ratio.

2. Taxable Capacity and Tax Effort:

   - Determining the level of tax revenue needed for growth requires assessing a country's capability to achieve that level.
   - Tax policy must consider factors like income distribution, economic structure, and administrative aspects for a durable and equitable structure.

3. Composition of Public Debt and Income Tax Dynamics:

   - Public debt arises from borrowing, influenced by government integrity, wealth, and tax revenue capacity.
   - Income taxes evolve with societal development, facing challenges in the

collection but remaining elastic to economic growth.

4. Commodity Taxes and Tariffs:

- The design of commodity taxation poses questions about which products to tax and at what rates, requiring careful consideration of import duties and domestic taxation coordination.
- Taxing luxury consumption emerges as a solution to address income inequality and protect savings.

5. Tax Incentives and Expenditure Policy:

- Tax incentives and expenditure policy are critical factors in development finance, requiring a balanced approach to resource allocation.
- Effective design of tax incentives involves considerations for domestic, foreign, and export incentives, each tailored to achieve specific economic goals.

6. Government Spending, Investment, and Per Capita Analysis:

- Government expenditure policy influences resource allocation, with a significant portion directed towards education and health services in low-income countries.
- Gross Fixed Capital Formation (GFCF), representing government investment, plays a crucial role in economic development.

Fiscal Policy, Stability, and Growth

The pivotal role of fiscal policy in ensuring stability and growth in less developed countries (LDCs) is of utmost significance, particularly when considering macro aspects of the issue. Understanding the problem through the lens of a fully employed economy helps to explain how fiscal policy can help to grow the domestic savings ratio. While tax revenue is needed, the success of raising revenue through taxes depends on the institutional framework, tax administration capabilities, and the political will to enforce necessary assessments. Striking a balance is crucial to ensure the successful implementation of development plans. Borrowing from abroad provides additional resources for investment and allows for a lower tax rate and higher current consumption. Although the net gain for future generations is less than tax finance, foreign borrowing remains significant due to the additional income to the domestic economy.

Taxable Capacity and Tax Effort

Determining the overall level of tax revenue needed for growth is crucial, but so is assessing a country's capability to achieve that level. Tax policy should not be viewed independently of the economy's overall productivity. Among other things, consideration should be given to the level and distribution of income, the economic structure, and the administrative and societal aspects of taxation. A realistic appraisal must acknowledge a country's available "tax handles" and recognize that a durable and equitable tax structure requires more than short-term devices. Resorting to tax farming or revenue quotas to officials may help temporarily but cannot form the foundation for a sustainable tax structure. Additionally, the tax system has to evolve alongside the stages of development of society.

In most low-income countries, especially, the tax structure prominently features taxes on external trade (mainly customs duties) and taxes on domestic production and sales. As per capita income rises, the significance of income taxes increases relative to customs duties and domestic production taxes. Payroll taxes also gain relative importance with increasing per capita income. The tax structure and composition change in line with the development of society. For instance, income taxes in low-income countries are often capitation taxes, distinct from the personalized individual income taxes in developed countries. The so-called business income tax in these nations often resembles a sales tax more than the profits tax applied in developed countries. Despite challenges in collecting taxes from wage and salary income in LDCs, the income tax contributes around 20 percent to total revenue in Latin American countries. Difficulties persist in reaching capital income, but the income tax remains elastic to economic growth. Taxing business income, whether under a separate corporation profits tax or as part of the individual income tax, poses considerable challenges. When business accounting lacks the precision to measure profits accurately, countries often resort to presumptive approaches, which may involve presumptive profit margins on sales or other indices like floor space for specific industries. Overlooking the importance of improving presumptive taxation techniques, some tax reformers focus on technical refinements that may not apply broadly to the diverse business sector in LDCs.

Given the prominence of agriculture in most LDCs, land taxation remains a critical issue. Determining whether the tax should be imposed on the value of land, actual income, or potential income under full utilization is essential. Adequate land surveys are crucial, but their absence often leads to haphazard assessment methods. Apart from land revenue, taxing urban real estate and implementing wealth taxes of the net worth type become essential, especially with advancing urbanization. Progressive taxation of residential property and wealth taxation can complement income taxation for capital income.

Commodity Taxes and Tariffs

The design of commodity taxation raises questions about which products to tax, at what rates, at what stages these taxes should be imposed, and how domestic product taxation should relate to import duties. Taxing luxury consumption emerges as a viable solution to taxing to address unequal income distribution and protect savings. Implementing progressive consumption taxation requires a system of sales taxation with varying rates based on differing income elasticities of products. Coordinating domestic excises with import duties is necessary, and a careful review of tariff policy is crucial. Luxury tariffs, often imposed to protect domestic substitutes, should align with corresponding excises on domestically produced luxury goods. Excluding domestically used capital goods from customs duties may contribute to price distortion and requires critical evaluation.

Tax Incentives and Expenditure Policy

In development finance, two crucial factors demand consideration: tax incentives and expenditure policy. These factors play a pivotal role in determining the resources available to the government for development purposes.

Tax Incentives: The twin goals of fostering economic growth and reducing inequality find their best realization through progressive consumption taxes and taxation of capital income under a progressive income tax. However, the potential conflict between the latter and investment incentives has led to thoroughly exploring methods to mitigate detrimental effects. Providing tax relief for investments that need to generate additional growth results in less revenue without gain and exacerbates income distribution inequality by favoring the high-income bracket. While past experiences suggest that tax incentives for investment have often been wasteful and inequitable, a blanket rejection of all incentive mechanisms is not justified. Political pressures will persist, making it pragmatic to design incentives as efficiently as possible.

Domestic Incentives: It is beneficial to distinguish between domestic incentives and foreign capital-related ones. Domestic incentives may pertain to general investments or be limited to specific industries or regions. Additionally, incentives might be crafted to stimulate exports and enhance the balance of payments. While general investment incentives, such as investment credits or accelerated depreciation, have questionable effectiveness, targeted incentives for particular sectors or industries may prove more impactful. The challenge lies in judiciously selecting industries that play a strategic role in development. However, the effectiveness of these selective incentives often needs to be improved. The list of eligible industries may need more specificity, and the selection process may succumb to political pressures or sustain markets for public enterprises that should not have been initiated. Despite the theoretical soundness of selective incentives, their practical application still needs to be improved.

Incentives for Foreign Capital: Foreign capital's role in development neces-sitates thoughtful tax incentives to channel it toward uses most beneficial for the entire country. Unlike incentives for domestic capital, tax relief for foreign investors requires a careful balancing act. The loss of revenue from tax relief granted to foreign investors should be outweighed by gains from additional capital influx. Aligning incentives with the domestic value induced by foreign capital is crucial. One potential approach to make incentives effective for foreign investors involves a tax-sharing arrangement, providing credits upon repatriation equal to the full tax in the Less Developed Country (LDC), even if a lesser tax is paid under the incentive arrangement. However, this approach needs incentives for reinvestment and may undermine the taxation of profits. The issue of competition among LDCs for foreign capital emphasizes the importance of cooperation to avoid self-defeating tax competition. Common market arrangements among groups of LDCs can play a crucial role in achieving this cooperation.

Export Incentives: Tax incentives for exports are widely used to assist in foreign market development and strengthen the balance of payments. To be effective, these incentives should be tied not to total foreign sales or profits but to domestic value added. Focusing on the latter component ensures that only the value added domestically contributes to the country's foreign exchange earnings, preventing the re-export of imported material or intermediate goods from distorting the incentives.

Tax Laws and Administration in Nigeria

Nigeria's tax laws have diverse sources, including legislation, the federal constitution, court judgments, circulars, and practices of inland revenue officials. The primary legislative sources include laws governing Personal Income Tax, Company Taxation, Capital Taxation, Petroleum Profit Taxation, Consumption Taxation, and Education Tax. The administration of these taxes involves various tax authorities, such as the Federal Board of Inland Revenue (FBIR), State Internal Revenue Board (SIRB), and Local Government Revenue

Committee.

Key tax laws in Nigeria cover personal income tax (PITA), company income tax (CITA), petroleum profits tax (PPTA), value-added tax (VAT), stamp duties, education tax, and capital gain tax. Each law specifies the tax treatment for different categories of income or transactions. For instance, PITA addresses individual and partnership incomes, while CITA focuses on corporate incomes.

Local Government Revenue Committee: Established under section 90 of PITA, the Local Government Revenue Committee (LGRC) is mandated to facilitate the assessment and collection of taxes, fines, and rates within its jurisdiction. The committee operates independently of the local government treasury department and oversees its day-to-day administration.

Joint Tax Board (JTB): Section 86 of PITA outlines the establishment of the JTB, chaired by the FBIR chairman. Comprising members from SBIR, a secretary appointed by the Federal Civil Service Commission, and the legal adviser of FIRS, the JTB holds functions such as exercising powers conferred by PITA, advising on double taxation arrangements, recommending rates of capital allowances, promoting uniformity in tax application, and imposing decisions on procedural matters.

Joint State Revenue Committee (JSRC): Section 92 of PITA establishes the JSRC for each state. Chaired by the SIRS chairman, the committee includes representatives from LGRC, the Bureau for Local Government Affairs, RMAFC, FRSC, the legal adviser of SIRS, and the committee secretary. The JSRC implements JTB decisions, advises on revenue matters, harmonizes tax administration, enlightens the public on revenue issues, and carries out additional functions assigned by the JTB.

Tax Jurisdictions: Taxes collected by the Federal Government through FBIR include Companies' Income Tax, Withholding Tax, Petroleum Profits Tax, VAT, Education Tax, Capital Gains Tax, and Stamp Duties. Taxes and levies collected by State Governments through SBIR cover PAYE, direct taxation, stamp duties, pool, betting, lottery, and road taxes. Local Governments collect taxes and levies like shop and kiosk rates, liquor license fees, marriage and birth registration fees, market levies, and permits.

Expenditure Policy

While tax policy has been extensively studied in economic development, expenditure policy, crucial for resource allocation in government, has received comparatively less attention. Comparing the expenditure patterns of African, Latin American, and Asian countries with European counterparts provides some insights. In low-income countries, a larger portion of expenditures is directed towards education and health services. In contrast, high-income countries allocate more to transfers, reflecting the development of social security system variations. Public investment plays a strategic role in economic development due to underdeveloped private capital markets, local entrepreneurial talent scarcity, and the need for significant initial investments in infrastructure projects.

Cost-benefit analysis becomes crucial in ensuring efficient resource utilization in developing countries. The analysis is simpler in these contexts as public investment often targets intermediate goods, facilitating measurement of their impact on the prices of privately provided goods. Determining the discount rate poses challenges, with considerations for external benefits suggesting a social rate below-prevailing market rates. However, issues like the high cost of forgoing current consumption at low-income levels complicate rate determination. Human investment, particularly in education, plays a critical role in development. Efficient education programs tailored to meet specific labor skill needs are essential for equitable distribution of gains from economic growth.

Government spending involves allocating funds by the public sector to acquire goods and provide services, encompassing areas such as education, healthcare, social protection, and defense. Government spending can be classified as:

1. Government Final Consumption Spending: In national income accounting, this pertains to acquiring goods and services for immediate use, satisfying individual or collective needs.
2. Government Investment: This category involves acquiring goods and

services for future use, including public consumption and investment, and transfer payments like income transfers.

Evolution of Public Spending

In the 20th century, public spending was substantially increased globally, with governments focusing more on sectors like education, healthcare, and social protection. However, governments globally rely on the private sector to produce and manage goods and services, often utilizing public-private partnerships to finance infrastructure projects. Public-private partnerships, especially in low and middle-income countries, have significantly increased in value, showcasing a shift in collaboration dynamics. Governments commonly supply goods and services not provided by the private sector, such as defense, roads, hospitals, and schools, improving the supply side of the macro-economy through investments in human capital development, providing subsidies to industries requiring financial support for operation or expansion, and redistributing income and promoting social welfare.

Theories of Public Expenditure

Theories of public expenditure are guided by principles like the "canons of public expenditure," emphasizing factors such as Benefit, economy, sanction, and surplus. Canons like Benefit (maximizing social benefits), Economy (productive and efficient spending), Sanction (authorized expenditure), and Surplus (ensuring revenue exceeds expenditure). Additional canons include elasticity, productivity, and equitable distribution, contributing to efficient and balanced expenditure policies. Moreover, understanding government spending involves navigating its classifications, historical trends, collaborative models, purposes, types, financing methods, and guiding principles around economic theories. Government expenditure can impact on the economy in various ways.

Crowding Out Effect: The potential shift of resources from the private sector to the public sector due to increased government deficit spending is termed crowding out. The crowding-out effect occurs when an increase in government deficit spending leads to the "crowding out" of private investment, as the government's actions raise interest rates and reduce the capital available to the private sector. Government spending serves as a potent economic policy tool. Given an initial equilibrium, if the government increases deficit spending, it borrows from the private capital market, reducing the supply of savings. The new equilibrium sees an increased interest rate and decreased capital available to the private sector. Thus, the government makes borrowing more expensive, crowding out some private investment and potentially limiting economic growth.

Expansionary Fiscal Policy: This involves increasing government spending or decreasing taxes to stimulate the economy during a recession, boosting demand for goods and services, and increasing output and employment.

Contractionary Fiscal Policy: Involves decreasing government spending or increasing taxes to cool down an overheated economy during a boom, helping to curb inflation.

During economic downturns, changes in government spending can occur through two mechanisms:

1. Automatic Stabilization: Existing policies automatically adjust government spending or taxes in response to economic changes without requiring new laws. Examples include Unemployment Insurance and providing financial assistance to the unemployed.
2. Discretionary Stabilization: Governments take deliberate actions, passing new laws to adjust government spending or taxes directly responding to economic shifts. For instance, increasing government spending during a recession.

John Maynard Keynes advocated for government deficit spending in response to economic contractions. According to Keynesian economics, increased government spending boosts aggregate demand, leading to higher consumption, increased production, and a faster recovery from recessions. Classical economists, however, argue that increased government spending shifts resources from the productive private sector to the less productive public sector, exacerbating economic contractions.

Composition of Public Expenditure

Public expenditure can be categorized into COFOG (Classification of the Functions of Government) categories: Social Protection, Health, General Public Services, Education, Economic Affairs, Public Order and Safety, Defense, Recreation, Culture and Religion, Environmental Protection, and Housing and Community Services. Functionally, government spending can be divided into three primary groups:

1. Government Consumption: Covers purchases of goods and services, such as infrastructure repairs, national defense, schools, healthcare, and government salaries.
2. Investments: Focus on sciences, strategic technological innovations, and other public needs.
3. Transfer Payments: Involves payments to individuals without exchanging goods or services, including Old Age Security, Employment Insurance benefits, and business subsidies. Interest payments to holders of government bonds are also included.

The United States leads national defense spending, allocating a significantly larger budget than other countries. In 2019, the U.S. approved a discretionary military spending budget of $686.1 billion, nearly three times more than China, the second-largest spender. However, healthcare and medical research spending is prioritized in Australia, crowding in university life science research, where subsidies and government projects are justified based on a positive return on investment.

Gross Fixed Capital Formation and Government Spending

Gross Fixed Capital Formation (GFCF) is a critical aspect of government spending, representing acquisitions to yield future benefits, such as investments in infrastructure or research. Often referred to as government investment, GFCF typically constitutes a significant portion of government activities. Government acquisition of goods and services can occur through in-house production, utilizing the government's labor force, fixed assets, and purchased goods and services for intermediate consumption. Alternatively, the government can make purchases from market producers. In economic theory, investment involves purchasing goods not for immediate consumption but for future production, essentially capital. Examples include the construction of railroads or factories.

Infrastructure spending, categorized as government investment, is considered prudent as it saves money in the long run. For instance, spending on physical infrastructure in the U.S. generates an average return of approximately $1.92 for every $1.00 spent on nonresidential construction because maintaining infrastructure is usually more cost-effective than repairing or replacing it once it becomes unusable. Similarly, government spending on social infrastructure, such as preventative healthcare, can result in substantial savings. Preventative measures, like early-stage cancer diagnosis, can significantly reduce healthcare costs compared to emergency room treatments at advanced stages.

Per Capita Spending and International Comparisons: In 2010, national governments spent an average of $2,376 per person globally. However, this figure varied significantly among the world's 20 largest economies, with Norway and Sweden leading at $40,908 and $26,760 per capita, respectively. The U.S. federal government spent $11,041 per person. Other notable figures included South Korea ($4,557), Brazil ($2,813), Russia ($2,458), China ($1,010), and India ($226). It is crucial to note that per capita spending includes national, state, and local government expenditures. For instance, in the U.S., where 42% of GDP is spent and GDP per capita is $54,629, the total per person spending is estimated at $22,726.

Government Spending as a Percentage of GDP: The 2014 Index of Economic Freedom by The Heritage Foundation and The Wall Street Journal provides a perspective on government spending for various countries. Based on the United Nations System of National Accounts, these statistics include tax revenue for comparison. Public expenditures constituted 46.7 percent of the total GDP of the European Union in 2018. France and Finland led with 56 and 53 percent, respectively, while Ireland had the lowest at 25 percent. Social protection accounted for nearly 20 percent of the EU's GDP in 2018.

Transparency in Government Spending

There is an increasing emphasis on transparency in government spending, commonly referred to as "budget transparency" or "government spending transparency." This transparency aims to make public goals and expenditures more accessible. Studies suggest the need for greater attention to developing methods and evidence to inform the allocation of public sector spending between departments. Such informed decision-making can improve social welfare within existing budgets, ensuring public funds are optimally utilized. For instance, an investigation into funding allocations for public investment in energy research reveals insights into the past impacts of various drivers. These drivers include crisis responses, cooperation, and competitions, providing valuable lessons for adjusting investments in clean energy to achieve meaningful global decarbonization. Also, calls have been made for applying principles to government spending decisions systematically, considering current issues and goals such as climate change mitigation. Principles like "Public Money, Public Code" advocate for the development of software funded by taxpayers as free and open-source. Public sector ethics play a role in government spending decisions, influencing shares, intentions, and rationales while addressing concerns like corruption or diversion of public funds.

Review Questions

How does fiscal policy contribute to stability and growth in less developed countries?

What factors influence the level of tax revenue needed for growth, and why is it crucial to consider taxable capacity?

Explain the dynamics of income tax evolution with societal development and how it remains elastic to economic growth.

Why is coordinating commodity taxes and import duties essential, especially in addressing income inequality?

What are the key considerations in designing effective tax incentives for domestic and foreign capital, and why is a balanced approach necessary?

How does government spending influence economic development, and what role does Gross Fixed Capital Formation (GFCF) play in this context?

Discussion Points

1. Explore the challenges and benefits of implementing progressive consumption taxes to address income inequality and protect savings.
2. Discuss the potential impact of tax incentives on investment efficiency and income distribution, considering both domestic and foreign perspectives.
3. Evaluate the transparency initiatives in government spending and their role in informed decision-making for resource allocation, focusing on climate change mitigation and ethical considerations.

CHAPTER SEVEN: THEORIES, PERSPECTIVES, AND EVALUATION FRAMEWORKS PUBLIC EXPENDITURE

Summary of Key Points

1. Factors Influencing Public Expenditure Growth:

- Growth of Democracy, Population, and Price Levels: Democratic systems incur expenses in elections and maintaining institutions. Population growth demands spending on education and healthcare.
- Development Expenditure and Public Debt: Implementing developmental programs and rising public debt contribute to increased expenditure.
- Poverty Alleviation and Economic Growth: High poverty ratios and the pursuit of economic growth drive substantial spending.
- Wars, International Obligations, and Foreign Aid: Conflicts, global responsibilities, and foreign aid programs necessitate additional funding.
- Skepticism and Intervention: Growing skepticism about government intervention has led to a slow increase in the average public expenditure to GDP ratio since the late 1980s.

2. Theories of Public Expenditure Growth:

- Adolph Wagner's Hypothesis: Wagner proposed a link between economic growth and public expenditure, where the latter increases with rising per capita income.

- Peacock - Wiseman Hypothesis: Public expenditure increases likely due to displacement, inspection, and concentration effects.
- Critical Limit Hypothesis (Colin Clark): Imposes a maximum limit on government expenditure as a percentage of Gross National Product (GNP).

3. Canons of Public Expenditure: Alfred G. Buchler's principles guide government spending policy, emphasizing benefits, economy, sanction, surplus, productivity, elasticity, equality, neutrality, and certainty.

4. Framework for Public Expenditure Evaluation:

- Macro-Level Evaluation: Ensures consistency with macroeconomic frameworks to prevent rising deficits.
- Consolidation of Deficit: Comprehensive assessment of deficits across various public entities.
- Composition of Expenditures: Examines the revenue-expenditure mix for optimal outcomes.
- Criteria for Expenditure Choice: Evaluates efficiency, equity, and poverty alleviation objectives in expenditure allocations.
- Challenges and Application: Recognizes constraints in applying evaluation criteria comprehensively.
- Functional Composition Analysis: Analyzes economic imbalances and patterns of overspending or underfunding across capital and recurrent expenditures.

5. Historical Perspectives on Public Expenditure Growth:

- From pre-World War I to 1960, average public expenditure increased gradually from 22 to 28 percent of GDP.
- Post-1960, there was a surge, reaching 43 percent by 1980, with some countries exceeding 50 percent.
- In recent times, focus on infrastructure, healthcare, and defense, with

challenges like fossil fuel subsidies hindering sustainable energy transitions.

6. Analysis of Education and Infrastructure Expenditures:

- Education Spending: Focus on primary education due to social extremality, with challenges in assessing net social benefits.
- Infrastructure Expenditures: Changing dynamics in the public provision due to technological advancements, with challenges in assessing the impact on people experiencing poverty.

Public Expenditure and Economic Perspectives

The expansion of public expenditure has been a focal point in economic discussions in recent times. Economists like David Ricardo emphasized the need to control the budget for a peaceful government. Most modern states, whether originally capitalist or socialist, are evolving and transforming into welfare states, much in line with Adolph Wagner's "Law of Increase of State Activities," which highlights that increasing government activity is a regular occurrence in progressive states. The emergence of modern welfare states necessitates extensive spending to address the needs of the masses, create job opportunities, and implement other welfare activities. Also, security and modern warfare preparedness compel nations to allocate significant funds to defense. Other factors contributing to growth in public spending are enumerated below:

1. Growth of Democracy: The current form of democratic government is expensive, with costs associated with conducting elections and maintaining democratic institutions.
2. Growth of Population: The rapid growth of the population demands increased spending on education, healthcare, and other essential amenities.
3. Rise in Price Level: Inflationary pressures lead to higher government

spending on salaries, goods, and services.

4. Development Expenditure: Implementing developmental programs, such as five-year plans, incurs substantial expenditure.

5. Public Debt: The rise in public debt results in increased expenditure on interest payments and repayment of principal amounts.

6. Poverty Alleviation Programs: High poverty ratios necessitate substantial spending on poverty alleviation programs.

7. Economic Growth: Governments allocate funds to accelerate economic growth, aiming to enhance their citizens' living standards.

8. Increase in Public Revenue: As public revenue rises, governments are inclined to increase public expenditure.

9. International Obligation: Maintenance of socio-economic obligations and participation in cultural exchanges adds to the indirect expenses of government.

10. Wars and Social Crises: Internal conflicts, prolonged droughts, unemployment, earthquakes, hurricanes, or tornadoes may increase public expenditure for reconstruction.

11. Supranational Organizations: Creating supranational organizations, such as the United Nations and NATO, necessitates financial contributions from member states, adding to public expenditure.

12. Foreign Aid: Contributions to foreign aid programs by richer industrialized countries channel some of their increased public expenditure into international assistance.

Since the late 1980s, a growing skepticism about governmental intervention in the economy has led to a slow increase in the average public expenditure to GDP ratio. Countries like New Zealand, Ireland, and Norway have significantly reduced public expenditure.

Theories of Growth of Public Expenditure

Three key theories explain the growth of public expenditure:

Adolph Wagner's Hypothesis: Adolph Wagner proposed the "Law of Increasing State Activity," asserting a causal link between economic growth and public expenditure. According to Wagner, as per capita income and output increase in industrialized countries, the proportion of public expenditure to total economic activity also grows. This growth is extensive and intensive, with governments taking on new functions while enhancing the efficiency of existing ones. Wagner explained the trend as follows:

1. The percentage of outlay for government-supplied goods increases with national income growth.
2. Increased public expenditure is a natural outcome of economic growth and the ongoing demand for social progress.

Peacock - Wiseman Hypothesis: Peacock and Wiseman argued that public expenditure does not increase uniformly but rather in a step-like manner. They studied the United Kingdom's experience from 1890 to 1955, focusing on fluctuations in government expenditure. Their hypothesis includes:

1. Displacement Effect: Moving from an older level of expenditure and taxation to a new, higher level.
2. Inspection Effect: Addressing neglected problems due to war or social disturbances, leading to increased obligations.
3. Concentration Effect: Central government economic activities become a larger proportion of public sector economic activity during economic growth.

Critical Limit Hypothesis (Colin Clark): Colin Clark's hypothesis is centered around the tolerance level of taxation, establishing a maximum limit of 25% of Gross National Product (GNP). Beyond this limit, an excess share of government expenditure in GNP leads to inflation even with a balanced budget.

Canons of Public Expenditure

Alfred G. Buchler outlined fundamental rules for using public expenditure, often called Canons or principles, to guide government spending policy.

1. Canon of Benefit: Public expenditure should maximize social advantage and welfare for the entire community. Resources must be distributed to increase production, reduce income inequalities, and enhance social life.
2. Canon of Economy: The state should be economical, avoiding excessive spending to prevent extravagance and corruption. Project appraisal and cost-benefit analysis should be conducted to minimize social costs.
3. Canon of Sanction: Every expenditure should occur with proper approval. Spending authorities must adhere to approved amounts, and public accounts should be audited to prevent arbitrary spending.
4. Canon of Surplus: Advocates for the avoidance of deficits in public expenditure. Balanced budgets are preferable, but modern governments may consider surplus budgets in inflationary conditions.
5. Canon of Productivity: Public expenditure should promote production, focusing on developmental activities to maximize production, employment, and income.
6. Canon of Elasticity: There should be flexibility in government expenditure to adapt to changing conditions, increasing during emergencies and reducing during normalcy.
7. Canon of Equality: Public expenditure should aim to reduce inequality in income distribution, benefitting the poorer sections of society.
8. Canon of Neutrality: Public expenditure should not worsen the production-distribution-exchange relationship, aiming for increased production, reduced inequality, and improved economic activity.
9. Canon of Certainty: Public authorities should clearly understand the purposes and extent of public expenditure, emphasizing the preparation of public budgets.

In summary, these theories and canons provide a comprehensive framework for understanding the growth and effective utilization of public expenditure in the economic context.

Framework for Public Expenditure Evaluation

Evaluation has become critical in public resource allocation and management across numerous governments. Concerns over public expenditure allocation, particularly in developing countries, have intensified. Governments, compelled by macroeconomic imbalances to curtail spending, face challenging decisions in restructuring expenditure compositions to meet fiscal targets. Donors, whether directly or indirectly financing expenditures, are placing increased emphasis on evaluating public spending.

Macroeconomic Evaluation of Expenditure Composition

1. Begin by evaluating the aggregate level of public spending, ensuring consistency with the macroeconomic framework to prevent rising budget deficits.
2. Consider macroeconomic imbalances resulting from various financing methods, such as external borrowing, foreign reserves depletion, excessive money printing, or domestic borrowing.
3. Stable and low fiscal deficits correlate with higher growth, investment, and current account balances.
4. Calculate the sustainable deficit by projecting future debt to GDP, desired inflation rate, real interest rate, and economic growth rate.

Consolidation of Deficit

1. Assess the consolidated deficit by adding deficits of various public entities, including central and other levels of government.
2. Comprehensive consolidation is essential to maintain macroeconomic consistency.

3. Evaluate the social desirability of deficit composition, considering the role of government versus the private sector.

Composition of Expenditures

1. Examine the composition of the deficit, focusing on the revenue-expenditure mix.
2. Analyze the sustainable revenue, considering tax structure and minimizing distortionary costs.
3. Iterate between maximum permissible spending and social desirability analysis for optimal outcomes.

Criteria for Expenditure Choice

1. Assess expenditure allocations using three-step criteria: efficiency, efficiency improvement over the private market, and equity.
2. Determine the rationale for government intervention, focusing on addressing market failures.
3. Calculate the social cost-benefit of alternative expenditure allocations to maximize net contribution to social welfare.
4. Consider the impact on the poor through benefit-incidence analysis to meet poverty alleviation objectives.

Challenges and Application

1. Recognize the infeasibility of applying the criteria comprehensively due to information and capacity constraints.
2. Choose the level and scope of analysis aligned with available information, providing useful insights for expenditure analysis.

Functional Composition Analysis

1. Ascertain the constitutional division of functional responsibilities among

various government levels.

2. Analyze efficiency and equity implications of intergovernmental fiscal transfers to offset imbalances and spillovers.

3. Address the challenges of intra-sectoral analysis within sectors like health, identifying legitimate rationales for public expenditures.

This comprehensive framework offers a structured approach to evaluating public expenditure at various levels. It emphasizes the importance of macro-level analysis, consolidation of deficits, and detailed assessments of expenditure compositions within sectors. Balancing efficiency, equity, and poverty alleviation objectives, the framework provides a strategic guide for governments and donors navigating the complexities of public resource allocation.

Historical Perspectives on Growth of Public Expenditure

At the end of the 19th century, average public expenditure was around 10 percent of GDP. The share increased to nearly 12 percent before World War I. The war caused a global surge in public expenditure, exceeding 25 percent in severely affected countries like the United Kingdom, Germany, Italy, and France. In the interwar period, the average share of public expenditure increased, driven by factors like the New Deal in the United States. World War II anticipation further accelerated this increase. By 1937, the average public expenditure share was between 22 and 23 percent, twice the pre-World War I levels.

World War I significantly impacted public expenditure, leading to a global increase in its share of GDP. Countries heavily affected by the war, such as the United Kingdom, Germany, Italy, and France, saw public expenditure shares exceeding 25 percent. In the interwar period, the average share continued to rise, with the United States increasing its public expenditure through initiatives like the New Deal. The anticipation of World War II in the late 1930s further accelerated this trend. By 1937, the average public expenditure share reached 22 and 23 percent, doubling compared to pre-World War I levels.

From the onset of World War I until 1960, the average share of public expenditure in GDP experienced a gradual increase from 22 to 28 percent. The growth, fueled mainly by military spending during World War II, resulted in Spain, Switzerland, and Japan maintaining public expenditures below 20 percent of their GDPs. Between 1960 and 1980, the average public expenditure as a share of GDP surged from around 28 to 43 percent. By 1980, no industrialized country reported a share below 30 percent, with Belgium, Sweden, and the Netherlands exceeding 50 percent. While the growth continued in the last two decades of the 20th century, the pace slowed. In 1996, the average public expenditure reached approximately 45 percent, showcasing a slower increase compared to the period from 1960 to 1980. Interestingly, during the 1980-1996 period, some countries experienced a decline in the share of public expenditure, including the United Kingdom, Belgium, and the Netherlands.

In recent times, the focus of most governments has been on infrastructure, healthcare, and defense. Among infrastructures, sustainable energy is a key focus, with investments in electrified transport and renewable energy considered essential for the transition to renewable energy. However, fossil fuel funding and subsidies remain a barrier to this transition. As governments navigate complex funding decisions, research, assessments, and ethical considerations are crucial in ensuring optimal resource allocation. The evolving landscape of government spending requires a balance between historical perspectives, current challenges, and future-oriented investments in sustainable energy and public welfare.

Analysis of Education and Infrastructure Expenditures

Education Spending: Various instructional levels—primary, secondary, and tertiary, along with vocational and technical education—emerge as major programs for analysis. Each level exhibits distinct market failures, benefits, and impacts on the impoverished. Recognizing the substantial externalities linked to female primary education, it should constitute a crucial unit of analysis, contingent on available data. The first criterion for expenditure choice underscores the more compelling rationale for government intervention in primary education, given the significant social extremality of basic literacy. Cost-benefit analysis, commonly applied based on wage differentials, faces challenges in measuring net additional social benefits. Studies on expenditure incidence consistently highlight the pro-poor nature of primary and secondary education expenditures over tertiary education.

Infrastructure Expenditures: In the infrastructure domain, spanning public utilities, public works, and transport services, the public sector traditionally played a dominant role in financing and delivery. However, there are changing dynamics in certain infrastructure subsectors due to technological advancements and shifts in regulatory management. A detailed analysis of the road sector illustrates the identification of major road types based on underlying market failures. Rural and uncongested inter-urban roads, as non-excludable and non-rival public goods, justify public provision. However, assessing the impact on people with low incomes remains challenging due to the public goods characteristics of roads.

Analyzing Intersectoral and Inter-program Allocations: Intersectoral allocations are evaluated by examining their correlation with economic growth through cross-country, time-series regression analysis. However, consensus on the impact of key expenditure categories, such as health, education, and transport, still needs to be discovered. Controversy surrounds the presumed negative impact of defense spending, with studies indicating a quadratic relationship between military spending and growth. The first step in intersectoral or inter-program allocation should prioritize programs the private sector cannot undertake, guided by the comparative advantage of the private sector. The second criterion—cost-benefit analysis—presents challenges in comparing and valuing programs across sectors. A three-step analysis is proposed, involving identifying alternative program combinations, selecting socially desirable outcomes, and evaluating tradeoffs between program expenditures and outcomes. While measuring benefits is intricate, sensitivity analyses can be conducted using plausible outcome values from studies elsewhere. Also, political feasibility comes into play through the budgeting process, where stakeholders implicitly place social values on alternative public goods bundles, simulating a contingent valuation survey. An integral aspect of this analysis is explicitly evaluating the impact on the poor, emphasizing the cost-effective alignment of program expenditures with poverty alleviation objectives. Analyzing education programs and infrastructure expenditures provides a structured framework for governments and policymakers, guiding them through the complexities of public resource allocation.

Analysis of Economic Composition and Institutional Arrangements in Public Spending

In this context, it is crucial to address economic imbalances, including patterns of overspending or underfunding across capital investments and current or recurrent expenditures. These expenditures cover wages and salaries, other goods and services, interest payments, and subsidies. Underlying challenges involve biases towards new capital investments, insufficient funding for non-wage aspects, and instances of overstaffing with poorly compensated civil service. An integrated analysis of economic composition within major programs is essential to rectify these issues, involving collecting data, eliminating unproductive programs, and examining the balance between capital and recurrent and wage and non-wage components within each program.

The assessment of civil service wages and salaries entails examining total wage bills, civil service employment, and pay structures. Indicators such as personnel expenditures to total revenues or GDP ratios are used for a broad assessment. A more meaningful evaluation involves scrutinizing whether there is excessive public employment or unwarranted pay scales. Analyzing civil service pay necessitates considering nonmonetary allowances, comparing trends, and benchmarking against the private sector. Reforms aiming at efficiency and effectiveness have focused on reducing employment, decompressing salary scales, and incorporating allowances into monetary pay.

Evaluating non-wage pay is integral to analyzing economic composition within major programs. Reductions in these expenditures have often led to a skewed wage/non-wage balance and a decline in infrastructure and services. This analysis relies on information related to activity costs. Each type of subsidy and transfer must undergo separate economic evaluations.

Also, improving public expenditure allocations requires evaluating institutional arrangements governing key decision-makers and the allocations themselves. Evaluating institutional processes, incentives, and supporting reforms are essential for sustained improvements. The focus is on the broader policy environment determining expenditure rather than individual allocations. Moreover, the analytical framework for institutional arrangements in public expenditure management aims to identify formal and informal rules influencing three key expenditure outcomes: aggregate fiscal discipline, prioritization of spending among sectors, and technical efficiency. Four theoretical problems—the tragedy of the commons, information asymmetry, incentive incompatibility, and perverse incentives from external aid—pose challenges, and institutional arrangements can mitigate them.

Addressing the tragedy of the commons: Mitigating the tragedy involves basing the budget on a consistent macroeconomic framework, articulating a medium-term vision, granting central ministries decision-making dominance, and establishing formal constraints.

Reducing Information Asymmetry: Reducing information asymmetry and high transaction costs requires mechanisms like revealing civil society demands, building consensus, ensuring transparency in the budgeting process, and instituting mechanisms for penalizing or rewarding the government for its expenditure allocations.

Managing Incentive Incompatibility: Addressing incentive incompatibility within the government hierarchy involves implementing a medium-term expenditure framework (MTEF) that provides line ministries with resource allocations based on strategic priorities. Accountability mechanisms, including financial audits and performance-based contracts, are crucial.

Dealing with Perverse Incentives: Perverse incentives from external donor assistance can be managed by ensuring donor projects align with sectoral strategies based on accurate information about social preferences and coordinated donor support.

Generally, establishing an ideal public expenditure management system requires certain preconditions, including a strong adherence to the rule of law, freedom of the press, and human capabilities. The rule of law ensures the effectiveness of institutional rules, a free press supports public scrutiny of budget documents, and human capabilities are essential for executing mechanisms like auditing and cost-benefit analysis.

Review Questions

1. What are the main factors contributing to the growth of public expenditure?
2. Explain Adolph Wagner's Hypothesis and its implications for public expenditure.
3. How do Peacock and Wiseman describe the step-like growth of public expenditure?
4. What are Alfred G. Buchler's Canons of Public Expenditure, and how do they guide government spending?
5. How has the average public expenditure evolved from pre-World War I to recent times?
6. Discuss the challenges and complexities involved in evaluating public expenditure at the macroeconomic level.

Discussion Points

1. How can governments balance the need for increased public expenditure with concerns about economic efficiency and avoiding deficits?
2. Explore the impact of skepticism about government intervention on

public expenditure trends, considering examples like New Zealand, Ireland, and Norway.

3. Discuss the challenges and ethical considerations in allocating public funds for sustainable energy initiatives amidst fossil fuel subsidies and global energy transitions.

CHAPTER EIGHT: COST-BENEFIT ANALYSIS, PUBLIC EXPENDITURE, AND DEBT DYNAMICS

Summary of Key Points

1. Cost-Benefit Analysis (CBA) for Government Projects:

   - CBA is a crucial tool for evaluating government investment projects, initially used for water projects and now widely applied.
   - Key steps in conducting CBA involve defining project objectives, analyzing benefits (direct and indirect), determining project costs, and applying discounting methods for long-term projects.
   - Three primary evaluation methods in CBA include Present Value, Benefit-Cost Ratio, and Internal Rate of Return.
   - Choosing among projects is crucial, considering capital constraints and alternative interest rates.

2. Public Expenditure and Government Intervention Logic:

   - Fiscal policy, involving government spending and taxation, is a potent tool shaping economies, with an increased role post the Great Depression.
   - Fiscal policies include expansionary and contractionary measures, each influencing GDP components (C + I + G + NX).

- Objectives include short-term stabilization and long-term growth, with responses during economic crises through automatic stabilizers and fiscal stimuli.
- Challenges involve the effectiveness of stimulus measures, concerns about sustainability, and variations in low-income and emerging market countries.

3. Impact of Public Expenditure on Economic Development:

- Expenditure policy's impact on economic development is more pronounced in less developed countries, where public investment plays a strategic role.
- Human investment, especially in education, is crucial for economic development, with a focus on cost-benefit analysis for efficient project evaluation.
- Modern realities necessitate expanded government roles, contributing positively to production, distribution, and economic stability.
- Public expenditure acts as a tool to minimize adverse effects on production, reduce inequalities, and stabilize the economy during economic fluctuations.

4. The Economics of Debt Financing:

- Government budgets balance revenue and expenditure, with surplus and deficit scenarios influencing the need for debt financing.
- Public debt arises from timing discrepancies, economic characteristics, and strategic financial planning, even in balanced budget scenarios.
- Public debt composition involves borrowing from various channels, influenced by government integrity, wealth, and public confidence.
- Borrowing is driven by the need to address emergencies, fund capital projects, and manage current expenditures, affecting economic dynamics.

Cost-Benefit Analysis and Assessing Public Projects

Cost-benefit analysis (CBA) is a pivotal tool for assessing government investment projects. Initially used to evaluate water projects, CBA is now widely used to evaluate the direct and indirect benefits and costs of projects and to assess the viability/feasibility of alternative projects. CBA studies are typically initiated within government departments for budget preparation or as ongoing programs to establish efficient expenditure patterns. The key steps involved in conducting CBA are as follows:

Statement of Objectives: Explicitly define the program's goals, ensuring alignment with societal objectives. A sharp definition of project goals facilitates effective CBA, even for projects with multiple objectives. Also, identify various approaches to attaining the defined goals, considering different facilities or construction methods. CBA aims to determine the relative benefits and costs of major alternatives.

Analysis of Benefits

1. Define benefits as the present value of contributions to objectives over time.
2. Address questions such as what benefits to include and how to value them.
3. Distinguish between direct benefits to users and indirect benefits or externalities accruing to others.
4. Direct benefits are computed based on the amount users are willing to pay. Consider difficulties in valuing certain activities and acknowledge imperfections in market competition. Recognize uncertainties about future conditions influencing benefits.

Determination of Cost: Define project cost as the value of resources utilized, considering direct and indirect costs. Direct costs encompass capital, operative, and maintenance costs, while indirect costs may include those borne by other governmental agencies or society as negative benefits.

Discounting: CBA is employed for long-term projects where costs are incurred presently and, in the future, while benefits accrue over multiple years. Due to time preference and interest rates, discounting methods are essential to adjust benefits and costs. Three primary methods of evaluation are employed in CBA:

1. Present Value of the Project: Involves discounting the net excess of benefits over costs (B-C) for each year back to the present year. A project is justified if the net present value (NPV) is positive.
2. Benefit-Cost Ratio: Involves discounting benefits and costs to present values and comparing the ratios. A ratio greater than or equal to 1 indicates profitability.
3. Internal Rate of Return (IRR): The rate of return equating net benefits over the project's life to the original cost. It ranks various projects based on comparison with a social discount rate.

Choosing Among Projects: In real-world scenarios, capital is limited, and projects are often mutually exclusive. Therefore, choosing among projects is crucial. The best approach is to maximize discounted benefits while adhering to capital constraints. The selection of constraints is significant, and an incorrect choice may lead to inefficiencies.

Alternative Interest Rates: Three alternative interest rates are commonly used:

1. Marginal productivity of capital in private investment.
2. Social rate of time preferences.
3. Government borrow rate without reference to time preference.

Each rate has distinct implications and is chosen based on the context and objectives of the assessment.

Public Expenditure and the Logic of Government Intervention

Fiscal policy, involving government spending and taxation, is a potent tool to shape and influence the economy. Post the Great Depression of 1936, governments have increasingly utilized fiscal policy to bolster financial systems, stimulate growth, and mitigate the impact of economic downturns on vulnerable segments of society. Pre-1930, a laissez-faire approach prevailed, but with the Great Depression, governments embraced a more proactive role. Policymakers possess two main tools—monetary policy and fiscal policy—to influence the economy. While central banks impact activity indirectly, governments directly alter the economy through changes in taxes, spending, and borrowing, affecting resource utilization.

The national income accounting equation illustrates how governments influence economic activity: GDP = C + I + G + NX.

Types of Fiscal Policies

1. Expansionary Policy: Increases aggregate demand through heightened government spending. Directly impacts GDP, influencing private consumption (C), private investment (I), and net exports (NX).
2. Contractionary Policy: Reduces demand through lower spending. Tightens economic activity.

Fiscal Policy Objectives

1. Short-Term Objectives: Addressing economic fluctuations, combating inflation, and managing external vulnerabilities. Macroeconomic stabilization remains a focus.
2. Long-Term Objectives: Fostering sustainable growth and reducing poverty. Supply-side actions may improve infrastructure or education.

Government Response during Economic Crisis: In times of economic crisis, governments employ:

1. Automatic Stabilizers: Operate automatically based on tax revenue and expenditure changes. Expansive during downturns and contractive during upturns.
2. Fiscal Stimulus: Discretionary spending or tax cuts to boost economic activity. Aims to counteract declines in private consumption, investment, and international trade.

Challenges and Considerations

1. Automatic Stabilizers vs. Fiscal Stimulus: Larger automatic stabilizers in advanced economies may reduce the need for additional stimulus. Discretionary measures may face implementation challenges and reversibility issues.
2. Weakness in Low-Income and Emerging Market Countries: Institutional limitations and narrow tax bases often result in weaker stabilizers. Crisis response may need targeted intervention due to limited resources.
3. Effectiveness of Stimulus: Depends on size, timing, composition, and duration. Policymakers tailor measures to the estimated output gap and consider multipliers, which are larger with fewer leakages and accommodative monetary conditions.
4. Concerns About Sustainability: High inflation or external deficits may render fiscal stimulus ineffective or undesirable. Sustainability concerns can lead to private sector counteractions, such as increased savings or offshore investments.

In summary, fiscal policy's dynamic nature requires policymakers to navigate various economic conditions, considering the effectiveness and implications of their interventions. Balancing short-term stabilization with long-term growth objectives remains crucial to effective fiscal policy.

Impact of Public Expenditure on Economic Development

The role of expenditure policy in economic development remains relatively understudied. However, in low-income countries, a greater portion of expenditures is directed toward education and health services, distinguishing it from high-income countries where transfers hold a higher share. This discrepancy reflects varying needs and the strategic importance of public investment in fostering economic development, especially in the absence of fully developed private capital markets.

The impact of public expenditure on economic development is felt more in less developed countries, where increased public investment augments underdeveloped private capital markets and a scarcity of entrepreneurial talent. Essential at early development stages, requiring substantial expenditures in infrastructure projects and creating external benefits necessitating public provision. Also, developing countries need cost-benefit analysis to ensure efficient project evaluation. Applied more readily due to the focus on intermediate goods provision, allowing measurement of their impact on privately provided goods' prices.

Human Investment and Education: Human investment, particularly in education, is paramount. Studies show high returns on educational investment, necessitating the design of educational inputs to meet specific labor skill needs.

Traditional Views vs. Modern Realities

Traditional views emphasized minimal state interference, but modern economies require expanded government roles. Evolution from minimal functions to welfare state principles necessitating increased public expenditure. The modern realities support the following as positive contributions of increased public investment, especially in developing countries.

Effects on Production: Public expenditure aims to minimize adverse effects on production, enhancing the ability, willingness, and efficiency of the population to work, save, and invest. Strategic expenditure on education, health, and infrastructure fosters economic development.

Effects on Distribution: Public expenditure reduces income and wealth inequalities. Socially desirable expenditures, such as those benefiting people experiencing poverty, contribute to a more just distribution of income and wealth.

Effects on Economic Stability: Public expenditure is a tool to stabilize the economy, compensating for deficiencies in effective demand during depressions. Keynesian principles recommend compensatory public expenditure during economic downturns and surplus budgeting during inflationary periods.

The varied impacts of expenditure policy on economic development underscore the need for strategic planning, efficient cost-benefit analysis, and a nuanced understanding of the unique challenges faced by developing countries. As economies evolve, public expenditure becomes a pivotal tool for fostering growth, reducing inequalities, and maintaining economic stability in an ever-changing global landscape.

The Economics of Debt Financing

The government budget operates on a delicate balance between revenue and expenditure. A surplus occurs when revenue surpasses expenditure, allowing the government to save and build reserves. Conversely, a deficit arises when expenditure exceeds revenue, leading the government to rely on past savings to cover the shortfall. Persistent budget deficits are often labeled as a fiscal disease, signaling a reliance on borrowing to bridge financial gaps. However, even in balanced budget scenarios, borrowing may still be necessary due to the timing misalignment between revenue and expenditure flows.

Causes of Public Debt

1. Timing Discrepancies: Governments may resort to borrowing due to timing differences between the inflow of revenue and the outflow of expenditure. Recurrent expenditures occur continually, and in certain years, even with a balanced budget, borrowing may be necessary to manage these ongoing costs.

2. Economic Characteristics: Economic fluctuations can lead to the accumulation of surplus in prosperous years to serve as a buffer in lean years. Deficits do not solely drive borrowing but can be a strategic tool to navigate economic variations.

Composition of Public Debt

1. Borrowing Channels: Public debt results from government borrowing involving entities such as the treasury, banking system, financial institutions, businesses, households, and individuals. The debt is formalized through binding documents expressing the government's commitment to repay a specified principal sum and stated interest.

2. Factors Influencing Lending: The ability to lend money to the government hinges on the government's integrity, jurisdictional wealth, tax revenue capacity, and public confidence. Borrowing is influenced by the need to address emergencies, fund capital projects (e.g., roads, electricity), finance self-liquidating public enterprises, and manage current expenditures in anticipation of increased future revenues.

Effects of Public Debt on the Economy

Emergency and Capital Project Financing: Borrowing enables the government to respond to emergencies like war or depression. Also, capital projects, such as infrastructure development, are funded through borrowing to stimulate economic growth.

Self-Liquidating Public Enterprises: Public enterprises producing goods with private demand may be financed to serve specific societal needs.

Current Expenditure Anticipation: Borrowing may be employed to cover current expenditures, with the expectation of revenue increases later in the fiscal year.

In summary, public debt, a crucial aspect of fiscal management, is driven by various factors, including timing considerations, economic characteristics, and the need for strategic financial planning. Understanding the dynamics of public debt is essential for policymakers and citizens as they navigate the complex landscape of economic governance.

Review Questions

1. How does cost-benefit analysis contribute to the evaluation of government investment projects?
2. What are the key steps in conducting a cost-benefit analysis, and why is choosing among projects crucial?
3. Explain the types of fiscal policies and their objectives in influencing economic activity.
4. Discuss the impact of public expenditure on economic development, considering the focus on education and human investment.
5. What factors contribute to the causes and composition of public debt, and how does borrowing affect the government budget balance?

Discussion Points

1. Explore the ethical considerations and challenges associated with conducting cost-benefit analysis for government projects, especially in sectors like healthcare and education.
2. Discuss fiscal policies' role in addressing short-term stabilization and long-term growth objectives, considering their impact on different

population segments.

CONCLUSION

As we conclude this captivating journey through "Economic Governance and Public Finance Dynamics," we find it more compelling to seriously consider the marriage of theory and practice in studying the relationship between public expenditure and economic development. Each chapter contributed to growing our understanding of how the resources of a state can be mobilized and utilized for the ultimate good of the citizens without placing excessive fiscal burden on future generations.

In our journey through public goods, we uncovered the intricacies of their transformative potential and the challenges of equitable distribution. The role of contingently public goods emerged as a beacon of hope in addressing economic inequalities, echoing the need for universal support and political feasibility.

Fiscal policy, a guiding force in economic landscapes, unfolded its multi-faceted nature—navigating allocation, distribution, and stabilization. We traversed the terrain of fiscal federalism, where the balancing act of revenue, expenditure, and equity took center stage. The chapters resonated with the voices of scholars and policymakers, offering diverse perspectives on taxable capacity, benefit spillovers, and the intricate dance of fiscal differentials.

The budget, a fiscal compass, unveiled its significance in resource real-location, redistribution, and stabilization. We explored the burdens and intergenerational equity entwined in debt financing, understanding how debt dynamics echo through time, influencing future generations. The quest for stability and growth led us through fully employed economies, taxable capacities, and the delicate balance of tax efforts. Public expenditure emerged as a powerful tool, shaping economic development, minimizing inequalities, and stabilizing economies in times of fluctuation.

Theories, perspectives, and evaluation frameworks illuminated the complex realm of public expenditure growth, guiding us through historical perspectives and contemporary challenges. We witnessed the evolution of public expenditure from pre-World War I to the modern era, where the focus on infrastructure, healthcare, and defense vies with challenges such as fossil fuel subsidies hindering sustainable transitions.

Our exploration culminated in a cost-benefit analysis, unveiling governments' strategic decision-making processes in shaping economic trajectories. The impact of public expenditure on economic development became palpable, emphasizing the pivotal role of human investment, especially in education.

As we close this facet of intellectual exploration, the echoes of economic governance and public finance dynamics reverberate. These pages' intricacies, challenges, and transformative potentials serve as a compass for policymakers, scholars, and curious minds alike. Our understanding of the economic symphony has deepened, leaving us with a profound appreciation for the delicate dance of forces that shape our societies.

Ultimately, "Economic Governance and Public Finance Dynamics" is a testament to the perpetual pursuit of knowledge, the exploration of economic frontiers, and the quest for a more equitable and stable world. However, the echoes of economic wisdom linger, inviting future generations to continue navigating the ever-evolving economic landscapes.

SOURCES

Fiscal Policy for Economic Development: An Overview Benedict Clements, Sanjeev Gupta, And Gabriela Inchauste https://www.imf.org/external/pubs/nft/2004/hcd/ch01.pdf

Chapter 23 - Environmental Taxation and Regulation A. Lans Bovenberg, Lawrence H. Goulder https://www.sciencedirect.com/science/article/abs/pii/S1573442002800271

Chapter 32 - What is a Sustainable Public Debt? P. D'Erasmo E.G. Mendoza J. Zhang https://www.sciencedirect.com/science/article/abs/pii/S1574004816000148

All About Fiscal Policy: What It Is, Why It Matters, and Examples https://www.investopedia.com/terms/f/fiscalpolicy.asp

"Fiscal Policy" Before Keynes' General Theory Marianne Johnson file:///C:/Users/USER/Downloads/SSRN-id3252526.pdf

Fiscal Policy: Taking and Giving Away Mark Horton, Asmaa El-Ganainy https://www.imf.org/en/Publications/fandd/issues/Series/Back-to-Basics/Fiscal-Policy

Expansionary and Contractionary Fiscal Policy https://courses.lumenlearning.com/wm-macroeconomics/chapter/expansionary-and-contractionary-fiscal-policy/

Expansionary Fiscal Policy: Risks and Examples https://www.investopedia.com/terms/e/expansionary_policy.asp

Monetary Policy vs. Fiscal Policy: What's the Difference? https://www.investopedia.com/ask/answers/100314/whats-difference-between-monetary-policy-and-fiscal-policy.asp

How fiscal policy impacts business https://gocardless.com/guides/posts/how-fiscal-policy-impacts-business/

Fiscal Policy: Economic Effects Jeffrey M. Stupak Analyst in Macroeconomic Policy file:///C:/Users/USER/Documents/public%20finance/2070328945.pdf

Tax and Fiscal Policy in Response to the Coronavirus Crisis: Strengthening Confidence and Resilience https://read.oecd-ilibrary.org/view/?ref=128_128575-06raktc0aa&title=Tax-and-Fiscal-Policy-in-Response-to-the-Coronavirus-Crisis

Fiscal policy and high inflation https://www.ecb.europa.eu/pub/economic-bulletin/articles/2023/html/ecb.ebart202302_01~2bd46eff8f.en.html

All About Fiscal Policy: What It Is, Why It Matters, and Examples ADAM HAYES https://www.investopedia.com/terms/f/fiscalpolicy.asp

A Monetary and Fiscal History of the United States, 1961-2022 alan blinder https://www.milkenreview.org/articles/a-monetary-and-fiscal-history-of-the-united-states-1961-2022

Interactions between fiscal and monetary policies: a brief history of a long relationship https://www.pse-journal.hr/en/archive/interactions-between-fiscal-and-monetary-policies-a-brief-history-of-a-long-relationship_7902/

Taxation https://www.britannica.com/money/topic/taxation

Chapter 2 Fundamental principles of taxation https://www.oecd-ilibrary.org/docserver/9789264218789-5-en.pdf?e=1703964323&id=id&accname=guest&checksum=91EDD7C1544E5D4777ECE5A320702571

The Theoretical Foundations of Regulation on Public Finances http://real.mtak.hu/146408/1/CEALSCEPhD02RegulationofPublicFinances2.pdf

Public Finance: Theory and Practice in the Central European Transition https://www.nispa.org/files/publications/ebooks/Public-Finance-Theory-and-Practice.pdf

What Are Public Goods? Definition, How They Work, and Example JASON FERNANDO https://www.investopedia.com/terms/p/public-good.asp

Public Goods https://courses.lumenlearning.com/wm-microeconomics/chapter/public-goods/

The rationale for public sector intervention in the economy https://www.lo

ndon.gov.uk/sites/default/files/gla_migrate_files_destination/rationale_
for_public_sector_intervention.pdf

Free Rider Benefiting from a common resource without paying for it
https://corporatefinanceinstitute.com/resources/economics/free-rider/

Free-rider problem https://en.wikipedia.org/wiki/Free-rider_problem#
:~:text=In%20the%20social%20sciences%2C%20the,goods%20of%20a%
20communal%20nature

The advantage of international fiscal cooperation under alternative monetary regimes https://www.sciencedirect.com/science/article/abs/pii/S01762
68096000122

Who benefits from international fiscal cooperation? The role of cross-
country asymmetries George Liontos a, Apostolis Philippopoulos https://ww
w.sciencedirect.com/science/article/abs/pii/S1703494923000026

International tax cooperation and capital mobility https://repositorio.cepa
l.org/server/api/core/bitstreams/e4d0935a-6ae8-4ba7-8430-c7601f8cb05
8/content

Case Studies of Fiscal Councils—Functions and Impact https://www.imf.or
g/external/np/pp/eng/2013/071613a.pdf

Chapter 7 Broader tax challenges raised by the digital economy https://w
ww.oecd-ilibrary.org/docserver/9789264218789-10-en.pdf?expires=17039
75653&id=id&accname=guest&checksum=410D401BCAC2A4DD84E56FC0E
D2A1892

Taxing the Digital Economy in Latin America and the Caribbean: What can
be done https://www.afronomicslaw.org/2020/12/09/taxing-the-digital-ec
onomy-in-latin-america-and-the-caribbean-what-can-be-done

Green Fiscal Reforms, Environment and Sustainable Development https://o
nlineacademicpress.com/index.php/IJAEFA/article/view/6/375

What Are Smart Contracts on the Blockchain and How They Work https://w
ww.investopedia.com/terms/s/smart-contracts.asp

Aging Populations and
Public Pension Schemes https://www.imf.org/external/pubs/nft/op/147/

Fiscal Policy David N. Weil https://www.econlib.org/library/Enc/FiscalPoli
cy.html

Do Enlarged Fiscal Deficits Cause Inflation: The Historical Record Michael D. Bordo Mickey D. Levy Working Paper 28195 https://www.nber.org/system/files/working_papers/w28195/w28195.pdf

Fiscal Policy Can Help Tame Inflation and Protect the Most Vulnerable https://www.imf.org/en/Blogs/Articles/2023/04/03/fiscal-policy-can-help-tame-inflation-and-protect-the-most-vulnerable

Public Policy Origins, Practice, and Analysis https://web.ung.edu/media/university-press/public-policy.pdf?t=1661449833017

What are the principles of good taxation? https://www.futurelearn.com/info/courses/public-financial-management/0/steps/14705#:~:text=The%20principles%20of%20good%20taxation%20were%20formulated%20many%20years%20ago,%2C%20certainty%2C%20convenience%20and%20efficiency

Principles of Taxation https://taxjustice-and-poverty.org/fileadmin/Dateien/Taxjustice_and_Poverty/Introduction/05_Principles.pdf

Taxes Definition: Type, Who Pays and Why https://www.investopedia.com/terms/t/taxes.asp

Classes of taxes https://www.britannica.com/money/topic/taxation/Classes-of-taxes

Analysis of Assessment Methods of Tax Burden: Theoretical Aspect file:///C:/Users/USER/Downloads/2089-Article%20Text-6378-1-10-20120807.pdf

Tax shift https://en.wikipedia.org/wiki/Tax_shift#:~:text=Tax%20shift%20is%20a%20kind,the%20redistribution%20of%20tax%20burden

Distributional effects https://en.wikipedia.org/wiki/Distributional_effects#:~:text=A%20distributional%20effect%20is%20the,cost%20allocations%20of%20a%20project

Government Spending https://corporatefinanceinstitute.com/resources/economics/government-spending/

Government spending https://en.wikipedia.org/wiki/Government_spending

What Are Some Examples of Debt Instruments? https://www.investopedia.com/ask/answers/050515/what-are-some-examples-debt-instruments.asp

What Is a Debt Instrument? Definition, Structure, and Types https://www.investopedia.com/terms/d/debtinstrument.asp

Government Debt Management: Designing Debt Management Strategies https://thedocs.worldbank.org/en/doc/194071527797532524-0340022018/original/GDM1backgroundnotes.pdf

How to design a stimulus package https://cepr.org/voxeu/columns/how-design-stimulus-package

Green stimulus after the 2008 crisis: Learning from successes and failures https://www.iea.org/articles/green-stimulus-after-the-2008-crisis

A Comparison of Selected Stimulus Packages in 2008 and 2020: investing in Renewable Energy, Sustainable Agriculture and Food Security, and Gender Equality and the Empowerment of Women for Structural Economic transformation https://unctad.org/system/files/information-document/osg_2020-12-18_StimulusPackages_en.pdf

The United States' Response to COVID-19: A Case Study of the First Year https://globalhealthsciences.ucsf.edu/sites/globalhealthsciences.ucsf.edu/files/covid-us-case-study.pdf

China's Policy Experience in Responding to Covid-19 Shock https://unctad.org/system/files/official-document/BRI-Project_RP24_en.pdf

The Origins of Greece's Debt Crisis https://www.investopedia.com/articles/personal-finance/061115/origins-greeces-debt-crisis.asp#:~:text=The%20Greek%20debt%20crisis%20is,over%20the%20next%20thirty%20years

The IMF and the Greek Crisis: Myths and Realities

Speech by Poul Thomsen, Director of the European Department of the International Monetary Fund, at the London School of Economics https://www.imf.org/en/News/Articles/2019/10/01/sp093019-The-IMF-and-the-Greek-Crisis-Myths-and-Realities

Chapter 1. Fiscal Politics https://www.elibrary.imf.org/display/book/9781475547900/ch001.xml

Policy Challenges for the Next 50 Years https://www.oecd.org/economy/Policy-challenges-for-the-next-fifty-years.pdf

But Will It Work?: Implementation Analysis to Improve Government Performance R. Kent Weaver https://www.brookings.edu/wp-content/upl

oads/2016/06/02_implementation_analysis_weaver.pdf

Cross-Border Impacts of Fiscal Policy: Still Relevant? file:///C:/Users/USER/Downloads/c4.pdf

What Is a Tax Treaty Between Countries & How Does It Work? https://www.investopedia.com/terms/t/taxtreaty.asp

Five common challenges with Operational Transfer Pricing https://www.deloitte.com/global/en/services/tax/perspectives/five-common-challenges-with-operational-transfer-pricing.html

Common Transfer Pricing Issues and How to Rectify Them https://www.vietnam-briefing.com/news/transfer-pricing-issues.html/

Regional Financial Cooperation https://repositorio.cepal.org/server/api/core/bitstreams/c5982d1f-ee4a-464d-8e51-d199b48391b3/content

The Coordination of National Fiscal Policies in the Context of Monetary Union https://www.europarl.europa.eu/workingpapers/econ/pdf/e6en_en.pdf

ASEAN-5: Further Harnessing the Benefits of Regional Integration amid Fragmentation Risks file:///C:/Users/USER/Downloads/wpiea2023191-print-pdf.pdf

Base erosion and profit shifting https://en.wikipedia.org/wiki/Base_erosion_and_profit_shifting#:~:text=Base%20erosion%20and%20profit%20shifting%20(BEPS)%20refers%20to%20corporate%20tax,the%20higher%2Dtax%20jurisdictions%20using

Cap and Trade vs Carbon Tax https://earth.org/cap-and-trade-vs-carbon-tax/#:~:text=While%20a%20carbon%20tax%20sets,the%20rise%20of%20global%20temperatures.

Which is better: carbon tax or cap-and-trade? https://www.lse.ac.uk/granthaminstitute/explainers/which-is-better-carbon-tax-or-cap-and-trade/

What are some ways businesses can incentivize sustainable tourism practices? https://www.linkedin.com/advice/1/what-some-ways-businesses-can-incentivize-sustainable

Practical incentives needed to help firms adopt green practices: official https://vietnamlawmagazine.vn/practical-incentives-needed-to-help-fir

ms-adopt-green-practices-official-69852.html

Green Credit Programme of India: Incentivizing Environmental Actions and Paving the Way for a Sustainable Future https://calculuscarbon.com/green-credit-programme-of-india-incentivizing-environmental-actions-and-paving-the-way-for-a-sustainable-future/

Taxing Cryptocurrencies file:///C:/Users/USER/Downloads/wpiea2023144-print-pdf%20(1).pdf

Social impact bond https://en.wikipedia.org/wiki/Social_impact_bond#:~:text=Social%20Impact%20Bonds%20(SIBs)%20are

Social Impact Bond (SIB): Definition, How It Works, and Example https://www.investopedia.com/terms/s/social-impact-bond.asp

Green Bonds And The Emergence Of Sustainable Finance In The Nigerian Capital Market https://tnp.com.ng/insights/green-bonds-and-the-emergence-of-sustainable-finance-in-the-nigerian-capital-market

Green Bond https://corporatefinanceinstitute.com/resources/esg/green-bond/

South Korea postpones 20% tax on crypto gains to 2025 https://www.forbesindia.com/article/crypto-made-easy/south-korea-postpones-20-tax-on-crypto-gains-to-2025/78341/1

The Current State of Crypto Taxation in South Korea https://www.tekedia.com/the-current-state-of-crypto-taxation-in-south-korea/

Enhancing tax transparency with blockchain technology https://punchng.com/enhancing-tax-transparency-with-blockchain-technology/#:~:text=Blockchain%20technology%20has%20the%20potential,reducing%20tax%20evasion%20and%20fraud

How we use data and analytics https://www.ato.gov.au/about-ato/commitments-and-reporting/information-and-privacy/how-we-use-data-and-analytics

Use of Big Data in Tax Administrations https://www.ciat.org/use-of-big-data-in-tax-administrations/?lang=en

Strategic tax management: best practices help ensure competitiveness https://www.dpc.com.br/strategic-tax-management-best-practices-help-ensure-competitiveness/?lang=en

7 Ways to Maximize Tax Savings with Strategic Tax Management https://www.nidhicpa.com/7-ways-to-maximize-tax-savings-with-strategic-tax-management/

What Are Tax Management Strategies? https://www.trilogyfs.com/tax-management-strategies/

Corporate Tax Planning and Financial Performance of Development Banks in Nigeria file:///C:/Users/USER/Downloads/SSRN-id3896368.pdf

Navigating the Nuances: Tax Planning with Legal Precision and Ethical Integrity https://www.linkedin.com/pulse/navigating-nuances-tax-planning-legal-precision-ethical-fdxec?trk=article-ssr-frontend-pulse_more-articles_related-content-card

Tax avoidance might be legal but it's time we seriously questioned its ethics https://www.manchester.ac.uk/discover/news/tax-avoidance-legal-ethics/

What Are Some Ways to Minimize Tax Liability? https://www.investopedia.com/ask/answers/040715/what-are-some-ways-minimize-tax-liability.asp

6 Strategies to Protect Income from Taxes https://www.investopedia.com/articles/personal-finance/032116/top-6-strategies-protect-your-income-taxes.asp

Business Taxation Meaning: Everything You Need to Know https://www.upcounsel.com/business-taxation-meaning#:~:text=of%20business%20operations.-,The%20meaning%20of%20business%20taxation%20refers%20to%20the%20taxes%20that,for%20adhering%20to%20tax%20regulations

How Does Corporate Taxation Affect Business Investment? Evidence From Aggregate and Firm-Level Data https://one.oecd.org/document/ECO/WKP(2023)18/en/pdf

Taxation of Income from Business and Investment https://www.imf.org/external/pubs/nft/1998/tlaw/eng/ch16.pdf

The Tax Advantage of Big Business: How the Structure of Corporate Taxation Fuels Concentration and Inequality https://journals.sagepub.com/doi/10.117

7/0032329220911778

Corporate Tax: Definition, Deductions, How It Works https://www.investo
pedia.com/terms/c/corporatetax.asp

Determining the impact of taxation on corporate financial decision-making
Savina Princen https://www.cairn.info/revue-reflets-et-perspectives-de-
la-vie-economique-2012-3-page-161.htm

Reclaiming corporate tax revenues https://www.epi.org/publication/reclai
ming-corporate-tax-revenues/

Tax Planning For Beginners: 6 Key Principles Explained https://www.botk
eeper.com/blog/tax-planning-for-beginners-6-key-principles-explained

The Principles of Proactive Tax Planning [Five Considerations for Business
Owners] https://warrenaverett.com/insights/the-principles-of-proactive-
tax-planning-five-considerations-for-business-owners/

Four Reasons to Align Your Supply Chain and Tax Strategies https://www.b
do.com/insights/tax/four-reasons-to-align-your-supply-chain-and-tax-
strategies

How do you balance risk and reward in decision making? https://www.link
edin.com/advice/0/how-do-you-balance-risk-reward-decision-making

Balancing risk and reward: How C-suite leaders can innovate responsibly
https://www.fastcompany.com/90977835/balancing-risk-and-reward-ho
w-c-suite-leaders-can-innovate-responsibly

Tax Planning Process https://www.stptax.com/tax-planning/tax-plannin
g-process/

What is tax planning? https://www.dsaprospect.co.uk/guides/tax-plannin
g

Tax planning process https://taxfitness.com.au/tax-planning/tax-planni
ng-process/

4-step process for tax planning https://www.farmprogress.com/manage
ment/4-step-process-for-tax-planning

Tax Credit vs. Deduction: What's the Difference? Both reduce your tax
bill—but in different ways https://www.wsj.com/buyside/personal-finance/
tax-credit-vs-deduction-6f611898

Tax Deductions & Credits https://www.investopedia.com/tax-deductions-

and-credits-4689689

What Is Tax Avoidance and How Is It Different From Tax Evasion? https://www.investopedia.com/terms/t/tax_avoidance.asp

Minimize taxes and maximize your bottom line https://www.investopedia.com/articles/stocks/11/intro-tax-efficient-investing.asp

Tax-Exempt Interest Definition and Examples https://www.investopedia.com/terms/t/taxexemptinterest.asp

Retirement Contribution: Meaning, Types, Limits https://www.investopedia.com/terms/r/retirement-contribution.asp

Tax Break Definition, Different Types, How to Get One https://www.investopedia.com/terms/t/tax-break.asp

How to get the most money back on your tax return https://www.investopedia.com/financial-edge/0312/how-to-get-the-most-money-back-on-your-tax-return.aspx

Tax Credit: What It Is, How It Works, What Qualifies, 3 Types https://www.investopedia.com/terms/t/taxcredit.asp

23 Income Tax Incentives for Investment https://www.imf.org/external/pubs/nft/1998/tlaw/eng/ch23.pdf

Understanding Business Expenses and Which Are Tax Deductible https://www.investopedia.com/terms/b/businessexpenses.asp

Deductible vs. Non-deductible Business Expenses https://www.sorgecpa.com/resources/insights/deductible-vs.-non-deductible-business-expenses

Ordinary and Necessary Expense: What it is, How it Works https://www.investopedia.com/terms/o/oandne.asp

Amortization vs. Depreciation: What's the Difference? https://www.investopedia.com/ask/answers/06/amortizationvsdepreciation.asp#:~:text=Amortization%20and%20depreciation%20are%20two,to%20reflect%20its%20anticipated%20deterioration

Amortization vs. Depreciation: What's the Difference? https://www.investopedia.com/ask/answers/06/amortizationvsdepreciation.asp#:~:text=Amortization%20and%20depreciation%20are%20two,to%20reflect%20its%20anticipated%20deterioration

R&D Tax Credits and Deductions https://pro.bloombergtax.com/brief/rdtax-credit-and-deducting-rd-expenditures/

Renewable Energy Credits (RECs), Explained https://watchwire.ai/renewa ble-energy-credits-recs-explained/#:~:text=So%2C%20What%20Exactly %20Are%20Renewable,power%20lines%20that%20transport%20energy.

Navigating the World of Taxation: A Comprehensive Guide https://www.lin kedin.com/pulse/navigating-world-taxation-comprehensive-guide#:~:tex t=Intriguingly%2C%20the%20considerations%20of%20residency,shape% 20the%20international%20tax%20landscape

Transfer Pricing: What It Is and How It Works, With Examples https://ww w.investopedia.com/terms/t/transfer-pricing.asp

International Tax Planning and Compliance https://www.hco.com/insights/ international-tax-planning-and-compliance

Guidance Note Compliance Risk Management: Managing and Improving Tax Compliance https://www.oecd.org/tax/administration/33818656.pdf

How Tax Treaties Prevent Tax Leakage in Cross-Border Projects https://w ww.huntonak.com/en/insights/how-tax-treaties-prevent-tax-leakage-in- cross-border-projects.html

Improving Tax Compliance: Establishing a Risk Management Framework https://www.adb.org/publications/improving-tax-compliance

Internal Audit and Tax Compliance https://myusf.usfca.edu/internal-audit

Internal Control System and Tax Compliance: An Empirical Analysis https://www.ijicc.net/images/vol11iss12/111204_Prawira_2020_E_R.pdf

Navigating Tax Risks in Indirect Tax: A Strategic Guide for Risk Management https://www.complyiq.io/navigating-tax-risks/

The promise and limitations of information technology for tax mobilization https://blogs.worldbank.org/developmenttalk/promise-and-limitations-i nformation-technology-tax-mobilization

Information Technology for Tax Administration https://pdf.usaid.gov/pdf_ docs/pnaea485.pdf

5 Tax Planning Examples https://www.modwm.com/5-tax-planning-exa mples/

4 global tax trends and how they impact your operations https://www.tm

f-group.com/en/news-insights/articles/2019/april/global-tax-trend-and-impact-your-operations/

About the Author

Professor Uwem Essia is a distinguished academic and celebrated author known for his illustrious career in leadership, management, economics, and development. Since June 2021, Professor Essia has immersed himself in personal studies and established himself as a prolific online book publisher, with a presence on platforms. He holds a PhD degree in Economics. Professor Uwem Essia's career is a testament to his passion for knowledge, education, and the betterment of society. His vast experience, research contributions, and dedication to fostering positive change make him a prominent figure in leadership, management, and economics. With a wealth of knowledge and a commitment to academic excellence, Professor Essia continues to make a significant impact. He is open to collaboration in joint research work/consulting, Adjunct and remote teaching, theses/dissertation supervision, professorial assessment, article/book editing and previewing, and joint book and article publishing.

You can connect with me on:

🌐 https://digitalgainspro.com

📘 https://www.facebook.com/uwem.essia.3

🔗 https://www.amazon.com/author/uwemessia

Also by Uwem Essia

Fiscal Dynamics in a Transforming Global Economy: Contemporary Issues in Public Finance, the Future of Fiscal Policy, and Projections for 2060

This insightful book delves into the intricate realms of public finance, the evolution of fiscal strategies, and the links between monetary and fiscal policies. Unravel the historical trajectory of fiscal policy schools, navigate the challenges posed by global shifts, and peer into the future of national policies amidst transformative landscapes. From strategic structural reforms fostering sustainable growth to projections for 2060 and beyond, this book provides a nuanced understanding of fiscal intricacies. A must-read for policymakers, economists, and enthusiasts, offering a holistic perspective on navigating the dynamic currents of our ever-evolving global economy. "Fiscal Dynamics in a Transforming Global Economy" is Book 1 of the Series titled "Public Finance, Fiscal Policy and Tax Management."

Principles of Corporate Finance

Principles of Corporate Finance, a comprehensive exploration and an enlightening guide, meticulously crafted for students and finance professionals, unveils the intricate layers of corporate finance theory, strategic applications, and ethical considerations. Each chapter equips readers with indispensable knowledge, from tracing the historical evolution of finance to navigating modern challenges like ESG integration, risk management, and financial crises. The book has thirty-eight chapters organized into ten parts that explore the various dimensions of corporate finance theory, practice, and impact. It delves into financial statement analysis, time value of money principles, and crucial decision-making strategies. Uncover the complexities of mergers, acquisitions, and value creation while mastering stock and bond valuation. Beyond theory, this book addresses the ethical dimensions of corporate governance, business ethics, and social responsibility. Whether as a student seeking insights or a finance professional navigating the evolving landscape, 'Principles of Corporate Finance' is our essential guide to understanding and using corporate finance concepts and tools in your studies/research and professional practice.

Tax Revenue Optimization, Efficiency, and Strategic Management: From Business Income Tax to International Cooperation

"Tax Revenue Optimization, Efficiency, and Strategic Management." is the second in the Book Series "Public Finance, Fiscal Policy, and Tax Management". This comprehensive guide navigates the complexities of global tax systems, from defining business income and tackling temporal dimensions to unraveling challenges in complex transactions. Explore asset taxation frameworks and finance leases and gain insights into international taxation strategies. The book extends beyond conventional topics, emphasizing collaboration, leadership, and efficient design in transforming tax processes. Budget and tax officials in the public sector, political and business leaders, and academics in the management sciences, economics, and public administration, and those taking professional courses in taxation and accounting will find this book a useful intellectual resource, unlocking the future of tax management in our ever-evolving global economy.